Map Key

P9-DNI-595

Other Titles of Interest

60 Hikes within 60 Miles: Portland, by Paul Gerald

The Best in Tent Camping: Oregon, by Jeanne Pyle

The Best in Tent Camping: Washington, by Jeanne Pyle

GPS Outdoors: A Practical Guide for Outdoor Enthusiasts, by Russell Helms

Hikers' and Backpackers' Guide for Treating Medical Emergencies,
  by Patrick Brighton, M.D.

**For other outdoor titles from Menasha Ridge Press,
visit us on the Web at www.menasharidge.com.**

Oregon

PAUL GERALD

MENASHA RIDGE PRESS

DISCLAIMER

This book is meant only as a guide to select trails in the vicinity of the Pacific Crest Trail in Oregon and does not guarantee hiker safety in any way—you hike at your own risk. Neither Menasha Ridge Press nor Paul Gerald is liable for property loss or damage, personal injury, or death that result in any way from accessing or hiking the trails described in the following pages. Please be aware that hikers have been injured in the Oregon area. Be especially cautious when walking on or near boulders, steep inclines, and drop-offs, and do not attempt to explore terrain that may be beyond your abilities. To help ensure an uneventful hike, please read carefully the introduction to this book, and perhaps get further safety information and guidance from other sources. Familiarize yourself thoroughly with the areas you intend to visit before venturing out. Ask questions, and prepare for the unforeseen. Familiarize yourself with current weather reports, maps of the area you intend to visit, and any relevant park regulations.

Copyright © 2007 by Paul Gerald
All rights reserved
Published by Menasha Ridge Press
Printed in the United States of America
Distributed by Publishers Group West
First edition, first printing

Text and cover design by Ian Szymkowiak (Palace Press International)
Cover photo by Ken Barber/Alamy
Cartography and elevation profiles by Tim Lohnes,
    Steve Jones, and Paul Gerald

Library of Congress Cataloging-in-Publication Data
    Gerald, Paul, 1966–
    Day & overnight hikes on the Pacific Crest Trail in Oregon/
        Paul Gerald. — 1st ed.
        p. cm.
    Includes index.
    ISBN-13: 978-0-89732-973-6 (alk. paper)
    ISBN-10: 0-89732-973-2 (alk. paper)
    1.Hiking-Oregon—Guidebooks. 2. Hiking-Pacific Crest Trail—Guidebooks.
    3. Oregon—Guidebooks. 4. Pacific Crest Trail—Guidebooks. I. Title.
    II. Title: Day and overnight hikes.
    GV199.42.O7G47 2007
    796.5109795—dc22

                                                    2006100491

Menasha Ridge Press
P.O. Box 43673
Birmingham, Alabama 35243
www.menasharidge.com

Table of Contents

SOUTH

CALIFORNIA BORDER TO MOUNT THIELSEN

CENTRAL

NORTH

Dedication

To everybody out on the trail, and to my parents, Barry and Marjorie Gerald, just because I love them.

Acknowledgments

This whole PCT thing, for me, started with my friend Corky Corcoran. He's the one who told me he was hiking across Oregon and asked if I wanted to go. That led to my quitting my job at an insurance company, selling off a bunch of my stuff, giving up my apartment, and spending four weeks in the woods. So, in keeping with that theme, I also have to thank Team Faino (Linda, Brian, Dylan, and Quinn) for being such fine hosts while I was between places. Steve Moellering helped make the hike fun, as did his wife, Diana, and our fine, fast-hiking friend Jenny Kolot. Special thanks must go to the Towanda Clan (trail names Crow, Sherpa, and Little Monster, known elsewhere as Willy, Trisha, and Ashley), who contributed car support, a roomy tent, packing advice, and limitless charm and loveliness. Craig Schuhmann was also instrumental, mainly by driving up to the trail to rescue us on a few occasions, and by loaning me a backpack when mine snapped. And when I had to get off trail for a while, the appearance of the Thursday Night Boys up in Three Sisters was special, as always.

As for researching and writing the book, it was a pleasure to share hiking and camping time (and an escape from a forest fire) with Jean Nelson. I enjoyed sharing "butterfly day" up near the Twin Lakes with Beth McNeil, and Jane Garbisch added her fine presence to a long day up at Lost Lake. Jim Sifferle pitched in some route advice for Chinidere Mountain, and the folks at **www.portlandhikers.com** helped in countless ways. And finally, Steve Queen of the Pacific Crest Trail Association took them time to read over all the text and maps; his feedback and suggestions made it a much better book.

And, finally, some fellow guidebook authors and their work must be acknowledged, because they helped fill in some gaps when I was sitting at my desk in November, wishing I had taken better notes back in August. Jeffrey P. Schaeffer and Andy Selters wrote *Pacific Crest Trail*, the definitive work for thru-hiking the PCT, and I leaned heavily on their Oregon–Washington volume. William Sullivan's *100 Hikes* series were helpful, as was Magen McMorris's *Oregon Hiking*. And if you see anything here about why a thing or place is called what it's called, that came straight from the incomparable *Oregon Geographical Names*, sixth edition, by Lewis A. McArthur.

And if I missed anybody, it's only because my brain doesn't work right. Too much time sleeping on the ground, I suppose.

Preface

It's usually about the third day of a trip when I start to feel comfortable. The first day I'm tired, the second I feel dirty, but somewhere around the third I start to adjust. My muscles get the hang of it, I get into the rhythm of the hiking life, and a plunge in a lake fulfills the purpose of a shower. That's when the Trail Mind kicks in, and from there on out, life gets simpler and simpler, the senses more and more open, the days grander and grander.

It's my sincere hope that this book will lead you down the same path. If you've never hiked much, or never backpacked, what you're holding can be a key to getting started. You can begin with some easy hikes, build up to an overnighter, maybe string a few together for a longer trip, and soon find yourself comfortable exploring Oregon's wondrous Pacific Crest Trail. Or not. You can also use this book just to day hike up to the highlights of the trail. And if you're an experienced hiker or backpacker, I hope this book will give you some ideas for places to go that maybe you didn't know about.

Either way, another goal of mine is to bring you a step or two into the world of the Pacific Crest Trail. It isn't just a trail; it's a subculture, a tribe, a way of life, a state of mind. It's a whole new way of looking at places. For example, we all know about Timberline Lodge, and we all know about Crater Lake. And we think of it as, say, a five-hour drive between the two. What I want you to do is see these places as a long-distance PCT hiker sees them: as about a two-week walk during which you will skirt the edge of towering peaks like Mount Thielsen, pass through glorious meadows near the Three Sisters, plunge into the lakes of the Olallie Basin, and slog over peak after ridge after butte. That's why, throughout this book, I've tried to tell you what a thru-hiker thinks of a place, or how many "trail miles" it is between points. Who knows? You might get so hooked you decide to hike all the way across Oregon; nothing would make me happier.

Writing a book is frankly not a lot of fun. Researching it? Sure. Driving around the state, writing off your expenses, going on hikes, camping out, dragging friends out with you, making new ones, seeing favorite places again, finding new ones . . . all wonderful. Sitting for hours at your desk, with the November rain lashing the windows and nobody around but you and the computer and a pile of notes, maps, and photos? Not so fun. Hurts the neck, too.

But as I write these chapters and sort through these photos, my mind wanders back onto the trail; it also has a fine habit of forgetting the fatigue, the filth, and the pain. I remember the butterflies swarming around the Twin Lakes, the waterfalls around Paradise Park, the clouds swirling around Mount Jefferson, the sunset from Observation Peak, the coyote at Timothy Lake, the elk at Crater Lake, and all the fine people I met along the way. Sometimes it all becomes a warm, comfortable blur that takes in the whole state—a single trail, a single experience that stretches from the Siskiyous to the Columbia River, all the way across this amazing state we're so lucky to call home.

That's the magic of the Pacific Crest Trail, and this book is an invitation to join me on that adventure.

Top 5 Hikes Lists

Most Scenic Hikes

7   Crater Lake Rim
11 Wickiup Plain to Sisters
    Mirror Lake
12 Obsidian Loop
18 Breitenbush Lake to Park Butte
23 Timberline Lodge to
    Paradise Park

Most Difficult Hikes

4   Sky Lakes Wilderness
8   Mount Thielsen Loop
9   Tipsoo Peak and Maidu Lake
23 Timberline Lodge to Paradise
    Park
27 Eagle Creek–Benson Plateau
    Loop

Easiest Hikes

1   California Border to
    Observation Peak
7   Crater Lake Rim
10 Rosary Lakes to Maiden Peak
    Shelter
19 Olallie Lake to Upper Lake
20 Little Crater Lake to
    Timothy Lake

Best-maintained Trails

10 Rosary Lakes to Maiden Peak
    Shelter

17 Jefferson Park
20 Little Crater Lake to
    Timothy Lake
21 Twin Lakes Loop
23 Timberline Lodge to Paradise
    Park

Best for Solitude

1   California Border to
    Observation Peak
2   Grouse Gap to Siskiyou Peak
5   OR 62 to Pumice Flats
9   Tipsoo Peak and Maidu Lake
25 Lost Lake to Buck Peak

Best for Children

10 Rosary Lakes to Maiden Peak
    Shelter
14 Little Belknap Crater
19 Olallie Lake to Upper Lake
20 Little Crater Lake to
    Timothy Lake
26 Chinidere Mountain

Wildflower Hikes

11 Wickiup Plain to Sisters
    Mirror Lake
12 Obsidian Loop
17 Jefferson Park
22 Barlow Pass to Timberline Lodge
23 Timberline Lodge to
    Paradise Park

Wildlife Hikes

Best for a Snowshoe or Ski Trip in Winter

Hikes with Dogs

Wheelchair Accessible

None, really

Steep Hikes

(Fairly) Flat Hikes

Introduction

How to Use This Guidebook

THE OVERVIEW MAP AND OVERVIEW-MAP KEY

Use the overview map on the inside front cover to assess the exact locations of each hike's primary trailhead. Each hike's number appears on the overview map, on the map key facing the overview map, and in the table of contents. Flipping through the book, you can easily locate a hike's full profile by watching for the hike number at the top of each page.

The book is organized by region as indicated in the table of contents. The hikes within each region are noted as one-way day hikes, loop day hikes, or overnight loop hikes (see page IX). A map legend that details the symbols found on trail maps appears on the inside back cover.

TRAIL MAPS

Each hike contains a detailed map that shows the trailhead, the route, significant features, facilities, and topographic landmarks such as creeks, overlooks, and peaks. The author gathered map data by carrying a Garmin GPSMap 60CS while hiking. This data was downloaded into *National Geographic*'s TOPO! program and processed by expert cartographers to produce the highly accurate maps found in this book. Each trailhead's GPS coordinates are included with each profile.

ELEVATION PROFILES

Corresponding directly to the trail map, each hike contains a detailed elevation profile. The elevation profile provides a quick look at the trail from the side, enabling you to visualize how the trail rises and falls. Key points along the way are labeled. Note the number of feet between each tick mark on the vertical axis (the height scale). To avoid making flat hikes look steep and steep hikes appear flat, height scales are used throughout the book to provide an accurate image of the hike's climbing difficulty.

GPS TRAILHEAD COORDINATES

To collect accurate map data, each trail was hiked with a handheld GPS unit (Garmin eTrex series). Data collected was then downloaded and plotted onto a digital USGS topo map. In addition to rendering a highly specific trail outline, this book includes the GPS coordinates for each trailhead in two formats: latitude/longitude and Universal Transverse Mercator (UTM). Latitude/longitude coordinates tell you where you are by locating a point west (latitude) of the 0° meridian line that passes through Greenwich, England, and north or south of the 0° (longitude) line that belts the Earth, aka the equator.

Topographic maps show latitude/longitude as well as UTM grid lines. Known as UTM coordinates, the numbers index a specific point using a grid method. The survey datum used to arrive at the coordinates in this book is WGS84 (versus NAD27 or WGS83). For readers who own a GPS unit, whether handheld or on board a vehicle, the latitude/longitude or UTM coordinates provided on the first page of each hike may be entered into the GPS unit. Just make sure your GPS unit is set to navigate using WGS84 datum. Now you can navigate directly to the trailhead.

Most trailheads that begin in parking areas can be reached by car, but some hikes still require a short walk to reach the trailhead from a parking area. In those cases, a handheld unit is necessary to continue the GPS navigation process. That said, however, readers can easily access all trailheads in this book by using the directions given, the overview map, and the trail map, which shows at least one major road leading into the area. But for those who enjoy using the latest GPS technology to navigate, the necessary data has been provided. A brief explanation of the UTM coordinates from Rosary Lakes follows.

UTM zone   10N
Easting   578410
Northing   4827494

The UTM zone number 10 refers to one of the 60 vertical zones of the Universal Transverse Mercator projection. Each zone is 6 degrees wide. The UTM zone letter "N" refers to one of the 20 horizontal zones that span from 80 degrees south to 84 degrees north. The easting number 578410 indicates in meters how far east or west a point is from the central meridian of the zone. Increasing easting coordinates on a topo map or on your GPS screen indicate that you are moving east; decreasing easting coordinates indicate you are moving west. The northing number 4827494 references in meters how far you are from the equator. Above and below the equator, increasing northing coordinates indicate you are traveling north; decreasing northing coordinates indicate you are traveling south. To learn more about how to enhance your outdoor experiences with GPS technology, refer to *GPS Outdoors: A Practical Guide For Outdoor Enthusiasts* (Menasha Ridge Press).

The Hike Profile

In addition to maps, each hike contains a concise but informative narrative of the hike from beginning to end. This descriptive text is enhanced with at-a-glance ratings and information, GPS-based trail-head coordinates, and accurate driving directions that lead you from a major road to the parking area most convenient to the trailhead.

At the top of the section for each hike is a box that allows the hiker quick access to pertinent information: quality of scenery, condition of trail, appropriateness for children, difficulty of hike, quality of solitude expected, hike distance, approximate time of hike, and outstanding highlights of the trip. The first five categories are rated using a five-star system. An example follows:

1 California Border *to Observation Peak*

SCENERY: ⭐ ⭐ ⭐	DISTANCE: *6 miles*
TRAIL CONDITION: ⭐ ⭐ ⭐	HIKING TIME: *3 hours*
CHILDREN: ⭐ ⭐	OUTSTANDING FEATURES: *Wide-ranging views*
DIFFICULTY: ⭐ ⭐	*from two vista points*
SOLITUDE: ⭐ ⭐ ⭐ ⭐	

The three stars indicate the scenery is relatively picturesque. The two stars indicate it is a relatively easy hike (five stars for difficulty would be strenuous). The trail condition is good (one star would mean the trail is likely to be muddy, rocky, overgrown, or otherwise compromised). You can expect to encounter only a very few people on the trail (with one star you may well be elbowing your way up the trail). And the hike is possible but somewhat strenuous for able-bodied older children (a one-star rating would denote that only the most gung ho and physically fit children should go).

Distances given are absolute, but hiking times are estimated for an average hiking speed of 2 to 3 miles per hour, with time built in for pauses at overlooks and brief rests. Overnight-hiking times account for the effort of carrying a backpack.

Following each box is a brief italicized description of the hike. A more detailed account follows in which trail junctions, stream crossings, and trailside features are noted along with their distance from the trailhead. Flip through the book, read the descriptions, and choose a hike that appeals to you.

Weather

The hiking season on Oregon's Pacific Crest Trail is like a window that opens briefly, and one must dive through it to take advantage. To carry the analogy further, one might even add that as the window opens (in July) and closes (in October), we have to be particularly careful, because July's lingering snow and swarming mosquitoes, and October's worsening weather can make a trip something other than relaxing and fun. Because it is first and foremost a *crest* trail, the PCT is covered with snow from early November to at least late June, though some of these hikes, in some years, will open up before that. Still, even in July, on the higher and north-facing slopes, you'll be walking on potentially a few feet of snow. In a nutshell, think of July as settling down but having bugs, August as being filled with flowers and people, September as being pretty much perfect, and October as offering fall colors and your last chance to get up there. That's our PCT hiking season.

When planning a trip at these elevations, even in summer, expect anything from heat to snow. As a rule of thumb, the temperature decreases about 3° with every 1,000 feet of elevation gained. Despite Oregon's reputation, there's very little rainfall, even in the mountains, in summer. As for temperatures, they can vary widely by location and elevation; what follows is a chart for Portland, which is near sea level. The Oregon PCT, on average, lies between 4,500 and 6,000 feet higher.

Average Temperature (Fahrenheit) by Month

	Jan	Feb	Mar	Apr	May	Jun
High	45	51	56	60	67	74
Low	34	36	38	41	47	52

	Jul	Aug	Sep	Oct	Nov	Dec
High	78	80	74	64	52	45
Low	56	56	52	44	38	34

Water

How much is enough? Well, one simple physiological fact should persuade you to err on the side of excess when deciding how much water to pack: a hiker working hard in 90-degree heat needs approximately ten quarts of fluid per day. That's 2.5 gallons—12 large water bottles or 16 small ones. In other words, pack one or two bottles even for short hikes.

Some hikers and backpackers hit the trail prepared to purify water found along the route. This method, while less dangerous than drinking it untreated, comes with risks. Purifiers with ceramic filters are the safest. Many hikers pack the slightly distasteful tetraglycine-hydroperiodide tablets to debug water (sold under the names Potable Aqua, Coughlan's, and others).

Probably the most common waterborne "bug" that hikers face is *Giardia*, which may not hit until one to four weeks after ingestion. It will have you living in the bathroom, passing noxious rotten-egg gas, vomiting, and shivering with chills. Other parasites to worry about include E. coli and cryptosporidium, both of which are harder to kill than *Giardia*.

For most people, the pleasures of hiking make carrying water a relatively minor price to pay to remain healthy. If you're tempted to drink "found water," do so only if you understand the risks involved. Better yet, hydrate before your hike, carry (and drink) six ounces of water for every mile you plan to hike, and hydrate after the hike.

Clothing

If you ever have a day to kill, just find a dedicated PCT hiker and say to him or her, "What do you wear out there, and why?" Technological advances in materials and the recent lightweight revolution in clothing and equipment have turned an already gear-happy crowd into complete gear geeks and "ounce police." You don't have to be this way, but there are some basics you should stick to.

The first thing to remember is *layers*, not *cotton*. Use layers. Don't use cotton. Cotton, when wet, will make you more miserable than you'd be without it. So go with synthetics and/or wool (which, if you didn't know, is now way beyond its itchy reputation). The idea of layers is that as you hike and rest (getting warmer and cooler), and as the weather changes, you can be prepared for any combination of movement and conditions. Some kind of hat is highly recommended as well.

As for raingear, if you're reading this, either you're an Oregonian or have spent some time here, so I don't have to tell you that hiking around here without raingear is like going to a barbecue without an appetite: downright foolish. I recommend something light (think layers!) but as waterproof as you can stand it—by which I mean something that isn't rubber but also isn't so "breathable" that you wind up getting soaked after a few hours of rain.

A result of the lightweight revolution has been that many long-distance hikers can now be seen in running shoes or other light footwear. More power to them, I say. I still prefer the stiff soles of hiking boots, and I need their ankle support to avoid twists and sprains, but this doesn't mean you have to wear the leather Herman Munster jobs of 20 years ago. There are fantastic, fairly light, waterproof boots out there that won't break your budget; just make sure they don't give you blisters (or that you've prepared for such) before you take off on some 15-mile adventure.

The Ten Essentials

One of the first rules of hiking is to be prepared for anything. The simplest way to be prepared is to carry the Ten Essentials. In addition to carrying the items listed below, you need to know how to use them, especially navigation items. Always consider worst-case scenarios like getting lost, hiking back in the dark, breaking gear (for example, a broken hip strap on your pack or a water filter getting plugged), twisting an ankle, or encountering a brutal thunderstorm. The items listed below don't cost a lot of money, don't take up much room in a pack, and don't weigh much, but they might just save your life.

WATER: durable bottles and water treatment like iodine or a filter

MAP: preferably a topo map and a trail map with a route description

COMPASS: a high-quality compass

FIRST-AID KIT: a good-quality kit including first-aid instructions

KNIFE: a multitool device with pliers is best

LIGHT: flashlight or headlamp with extra bulbs and batteries

FIRE: windproof matches or lighter and fire starter

EXTRA FOOD: you should always have food in your pack when you've finished hiking

EXTRA CLOTHES: rain protection, warm layers, gloves, warm hat

SUN PROTECTION: sunglasses, lip balm, sunblock, sun hat

Hiking with Children

No one is too young for a hike. Be mindful, though. Flat, short, and shaded trails are best with an infant. Toddlers who have not quite mastered walking can still tag along, riding on an adult's back in a child carrier. Use common sense to judge a child's capacity to hike a particular trail, and always expect that the child will tire quickly and need to be carried. A list of hikes suitable for children is provided on page XI.

General Safety

To some potential mountain enthusiasts, the deep woods seem inordinately dark and perilous. It is the fear of the unknown that causes this anxiety. No doubt, potentially dangerous situations can occur outdoors, but as long as you use sound judgment and prepare yourself before hitting the trail, you'll be much safer in the woods than in most urban areas of the country. It is better to look at a backcountry hike as a fascinating chance to discover the unknown rather than a chance for potential disaster. If you're new to the game, I'd suggest starting out easy and finding a person who knows what he or she is doing to help you out. In addition, here are a few tips to make your trip safer and easier.

- **ALWAYS CARRY FOOD AND WATER** whether you are planning to go overnight or not. Food will give you energy, help keep you warm, and sustain you in an emergency until help arrives. You never know if you will have a stream nearby when you become thirsty. Bring potable water or treat water before drinking it from a stream. Boil or filter all found water before drinking it.

- **STAY ON DESIGNATED TRAILS.** Most hikers get lost when they leave the path. Even on the most clearly marked trails, there is usually a point where you have to stop and consider which way to go. If you become disoriented, don't panic. As soon as you think you may be off-track, stop, assess your current direction, then retrace your steps to the point where you went awry. Using a map, a compass, and this book, and keeping in mind what you have passed thus far, reorient yourself, and trust your judgment on which way to proceed. If you become absolutely unsure of how to continue, return to your vehicle the way you came in. Should you become completely lost and have no idea how to return to the trailhead, remaining in place along the trail and waiting for help is most often the best option for adults and always the best option for children.

- **BE ESPECIALLY CAREFUL WHEN CROSSING STREAMS.** Whether you are fording the stream or crossing on a log, make every step count. If you have any doubt about maintaining your balance on a foot log, go ahead and ford the stream instead. When fording a stream, use a trekking pole or stout stick for balance and face upstream as you cross. If a stream seems too deep to ford, turn back. Whatever is on the other side is not worth risking your life for.

- **BE CAREFUL AT OVERLOOKS.** While these areas may provide spectacular views, they are potentially hazardous. Stay back from the edge of outcrops and be absolutely sure of your footing; a misstep can mean a nasty and possibly fatal fall.

- **BEWARE: STANDING DEAD TREES** and storm-damaged living trees pose a real hazard to hikers and tent campers. These trees may have loose or broken limbs that could fall at any time. When choosing a spot to rest or a backcountry campsite, look up.

- **KNOW THE SYMPTOMS OF HYPOTHERMIA.** Shivering and forgetfulness are the two most common indicators of this insidious killer. Hypothermia can occur at any elevation, even in the summer, especially when the hiker is wearing lightweight cotton clothing. If symptoms arise, get the victim shelter, hot liquids, and dry clothes or a dry sleeping bag.

- **TAKE ALONG YOUR BRAIN.** A cool, calculating mind is the single most important piece of equipment you'll ever need on the trail. Think before you act. Watch your step. Plan ahead. Avoiding accidents before they happen is the best recipe for a rewarding and relaxing hike.

- **ASK QUESTIONS.** National and state forest and park employees are there to help. It's a lot easier to gain advice beforehand and thereby avoid a mishap away from civilization when it's too late to amend an error. Use your head out there and treat the place as if it were your own backyard—because it is.

Animal and Plant Hazards

Ticks

Ticks like to hang out in the brush that grows along trails. Hot summer months seem to explode their numbers, but you should be tick-aware during all months of the year. Ticks, which are arthropods and not insects, need a host to feast on to reproduce. The ticks that light onto you while you're hiking will be very small, sometimes so tiny that you won't be able to spot them. They're primarily of two varieties, deer ticks and dog ticks; both need a few hours of actual attachment before they can transmit any disease they may harbor. Ticks may settle in shoes, socks, and hats and may take several hours to actually latch on. The best strategy is to visually check every half-hour or so while hiking, do a thorough check before you get in the car, and then, when you take a post-hike shower, do an even more thorough check of your entire body. Ticks that haven't attached are easily removed but not easily killed. If you pick off a tick in the woods, just toss it aside. If you find one on your body at home, dispatch it and then send it down the toilet. For ticks that have embedded, removal with tweezers is best.

SNAKES

There certainly are rattlesnakes in Oregon, but they're not 5,000 feet up in the mountains, and they aren't west of the Cascades, either. If you see a snake on any of these hikes, it will be a harmless and terrified garter snake, getting away from you as fast as it can.

RATTLESNAKE

OTHER CRITTERS

I hear there are black bears in Oregon, but in ten years of hiking, I've never seen one. And everybody I know who has seen one has reported the bears doing the same thing: running the heck away. Same thing with all forms of big cat, like mountain lions and bobcats, as well as elk—not that you'd be worried about elk. Especially if you're quiet, and it's early or late in the day, you might see the occasional coyote or deer, and at some point you will have the heart-stopping experience of scaring up a trailside grouse. Basically, there aren't any animals you need to worry about, other than the ones on two legs.

Poison Ivy, Oak, and Sumac

In Oregon, poison ivy, oak, and sumac generally don't exist above 3,000 feet—which is to say they shouldn't be a problem in the areas covered by this book. Still, some of the lower-elevation hikes, especially down south, might have them, so we'll go with the standard advice here. Avoiding contact with these plants is the most effective way to prevent the painful, itchy rashes associated with these plants. Poison ivy ranges

COMMON POISONOUS PLANTS

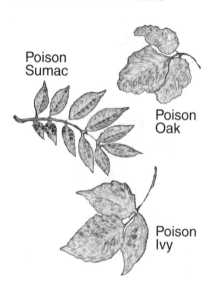

Poison
Sumac

Poison
Oak

Poison
Ivy

from a thick, tree-hugging vine to a shaded ground cover, three leaflets to a leaf; poison oak occurs as either a vine or a shrub, with three leaflets as well; and poison sumac flourishes in swampland, each leaf having 7 to 13 leaflets. Urushiol, the oil in the sap of these plants, is responsible for the rash. Usually within 12 to 14 hours of exposure (but sometimes much later), you'll see raised lines and/or blisters and experience a terrible itch.

Refrain from scratching, because bacteria under fingernails can cause infection and you will spread the rash to other parts of your body. Wash and dry the rash thoroughly, applying a calamine lotion or other product to help dry the rash. If itching or blistering is severe, seek medical attention. Remember that oil-contaminated clothes, pets, or hiking gear can easily cause an irritating rash on you or someone else, so wash not only any exposed parts of your body but also clothes, gear, and pets.

Mosquitoes

Oregon is known for rain, right? And the Cascades get a lot of snow? And when the snow melts, there's a lot of water around, right? And where do mosquitoes live? That's right, the Cascades. July is the Time of the Mosquito in the Oregon mountains, so if you're doing any of these hikes then, think seriously about long sleeves, repellent, and a tent. This is especially true of any high-elevation hike that mentions a lake in it (Sky Lakes, for example).

Although it's not a common occurrence, individuals can become infected with the West Nile virus by being bitten by an infected mosquito. Culex mosquitoes, the primary varieties that can transmit West Nile virus to humans, thrive in urban rather than natural areas. They lay their eggs in stagnant water and can breed in any standing water that remains for more than five days. Most people infected with West Nile virus have no symptoms of illness, but some may become ill, usually 3 to 15 days after being bitten.

Tips for Enjoying the PCT in Oregon

· WHEN YOU'VE READ A CHAPTER and are ready to hit the trail, it's best to make sure you can still go. Is the road open? Is the trail washed out? Is there a fire? That's why you should call the local national forest ranger district (see contact information at the end of this book) before leaving home.

- DON'T LET THE LISTED DISTANCE, or the elevation profile, for a hike discourage you from trying it. In almost all cases, there are fine attractions along the way, meaning you don't have to deal with that part of the profile that looks like a parking cone, or you don't actually have to put in, say, 21 miles to enjoy the Sky Lakes Wilderness.

- TAKE YOUR TIME ALONG THE TRAILS. Pace yourself. The forest is filled with wonders both big and small. Don't rush past a tiny salamander to get to that overlook. Stop and smell the wildflowers. Peer into a clear mountain stream for brook trout. Don't miss the trees for the forest. Shorter hikes allow you to stop and linger more than long hikes. Something about staring at the front end of a 10-mile trek naturally pushes you to speed up. That said, take close notice of the elevation maps that accompany each hike. If you see many ups and downs over large altitude changes, you'll obviously need more time. Inevitably, you'll finish some of the "hike times" long before or after what is suggested. Nevertheless, leave yourself plenty of time for those moments when you simply feel like stopping and taking it all in.

- HERE'S ANOTHER THING TO TRY: keep your head up. No, I don't mean "don't get discouraged"; I mean quit looking at the trail all the time. Sometimes, when I lead a hike, I tell people at the trailhead to take a good look at their boots, and then at the ground, and then I ask them to take my word for it that these things won't change. The views above, however, change constantly, and with a little practice you'll find you can trust your feet a lot more than you realized to get you over rocks and roots.

- WE CAN'T ALWAYS SCHEDULE OUR FREE TIME when we want, but try to hike during the week and avoid the weekends if possible. Trails that are packed on Saturday and Sunday are often clear during the week. If you are hiking on a busy day, go early in the morning; it'll enhance your chances of seeing wildlife. The trails really clear out during rainy times, but don't hike during a thunderstorm.

Backcountry Advice

In all but a few cases, no permit is required before entering the backcountry to camp. However, you should practice low-impact camping.

Adhere to the adages "Pack it in, pack it out," and "Take only pictures, leave only footprints." Practice "Leave no trace" camping ethics while in the backcountry.

Open fires are often not permitted, especially near lakes, in high-use areas and during dry times when the Forest Service may issue a fire ban. Backpacking stoves are strongly encouraged. You might want to hang your food out of the reach of bears and other animals to minimize human impact on wildlife and avoid their introduction to and dependence on human food. Wildlife learns to associate backpacks and backpackers with easy food sources, thereby influencing their behavior. Make sure you have about 40 feet of thin but sturdy rope to properly secure your food. Ideally, you should throw your rope over a stout limb that extends ten or more feet above ground. Make sure the rope hangs at least five feet away from the tree trunk.

Solid human waste must be buried in a hole at least three inches deep and at least 200 feet away from trails and water sources; a trowel is basic backpacking equipment.

Following the above guidelines will increase your chances for a pleasant, safe, and low-impact interaction with nature. The suggestions are intended to enhance your experience of the Cascade Mountains' flora and fauna. Forest regulations can change over time; contact forest ranger stations to confirm the status of any regulations before you enter the backcountry.

Trail Etiquette

Whether you're on a city, county, state, or national park trail, always remember that great care and resources (from nature as well as from your tax dollars) have gone into creating these trails. Treat the trail, wildlife, and fellow hikers with respect.

- **HIKE ON OPEN TRAILS ONLY.** Respect trail and road closures (ask if not sure), avoid possible trespassing on private land, and obtain all permits and authorization as required. Also, leave gates as you found them or as marked.

- **LEAVE ONLY FOOTPRINTS.** Be sensitive to the ground beneath you. This also means staying on the existing trail and not blazing any new trails. Be sure to pack out what you pack in. No one likes to see the trash someone else has left behind.

- **NEVER SPOOK ANIMALS.** An unannounced approach, a sudden movement, or a loud noise startles most animals. A surprised animal can be dangerous to you, to others, and to itself. Give them plenty of space.

- **PLAN AHEAD.** Know your equipment, your ability, and the area in which you are hiking—and prepare accordingly. Be self-sufficient at all times; carry necessary supplies for changes in weather or other conditions. A well-executed trip is a satisfaction to you and to others.

- **BE COURTEOUS TO OTHER HIKERS,** bikers, equestrians, and others you encounter on the trails.

South

CALIFORNIA BORDER TO MOUNT THIELSEN

Pacific Crest Trail: Southern Region

N

0   9   18
miles

138 Wilbur

Idleyid Park

Glide

138

Roseburg

UMPQUA NATIONAL FOREST

138

9

8

WINEMA NATIONAL FOREST

Myrtle Creek

99

5

227

Days Creek

Canyonville

Milo

Tiller

ROUGE RIVER NATIONAL FOREST

62

62

CRATER LAKE NATIONAL PARK

Crater Lake

7

Azalea

5   99

227

Lost Creek Lake

Prospect

6

5

SKY LAKES WILDERNESS

Fort Klamath

62

Trail

Shady Cove

62

Klamath Agency

Agency Lake

Grants Pass

99

Rogue River

Gold Hill

White City

Eagle Point

4   4
Nan Crk. Cherry Crk.

Upper Klamath Lake

140

Murphy

99   5

Central Point

140

Lakecreek

ROUGE RIVER NATIONAL FOREST

WINEMA NATIONAL FOREST

140

238

Medford

Jacksonville

238

Applegate

Phoenix

Talent

Ruch

Williams

Ashland

99

5

2

1

Siskiyou

3

KLAMATH NATIONAL FOREST

66

Keno

BEAR VALLEY NWR

ROUGE RIVER NATIONAL FOREST

OREGON

CALIFORNIA

1 California Border *to Observation Peak*

SCENERY: ☆ ☆ ☆
TRAIL CONDITION: ☆ ☆ ☆
CHILDREN: ☆ ☆
DIFFICULTY: ☆ ☆
SOLITUDE: ☆ ☆ ☆ ☆

DISTANCE: *6 miles*
HIKING TIME: *3 hours*
OUTSTANDING FEATURES: *A geographical curiosity, a quiet forest, and a sweeping, panoramic viewpoint*

If you ever wanted to say you hiked from one state to another, here's your chance. Enter Oregon the way northbound PCT thru-hikers do it, then climb the state's first peak for a lovely viewpoint—all without working too hard at all.

🚶🚶 Being something of a map geek, I had to tell people how to hike to the Oregon–California border. It's less than a quarter mile from a road, but that isn't really the point of this hike. Observation Peak is the point. And for the record, I would have included the walk from Oregon to Washington as well, but it's across the narrow Bridge of the Gods at Cascade Locks, with lots of traffic and no walkway. So this is your only chance at a border hike.

From the road, start south (right, as you drove up) through meadows and thin forest, for a quarter mile down to a register at the border. You can join the hundreds of others who have taken their pictures next to the "Oregon" and "California" signs on a tree, enjoy the views south into the Golden State's Donomore Meadows, and read the exuberant comments of the thru-hikers who have tromped some 1,600 miles just to get past one state. Most of them arrive here around mid-August, having started at the Mexico–California border around May 1. But their speeds vary greatly: on one September hike here, I encountered a northbounder who said he liked to "sleep late, nap after lunch, and have a good time." At the other extreme, I met a man at Washington's Snoqualmie Pass one August 30, then saw that

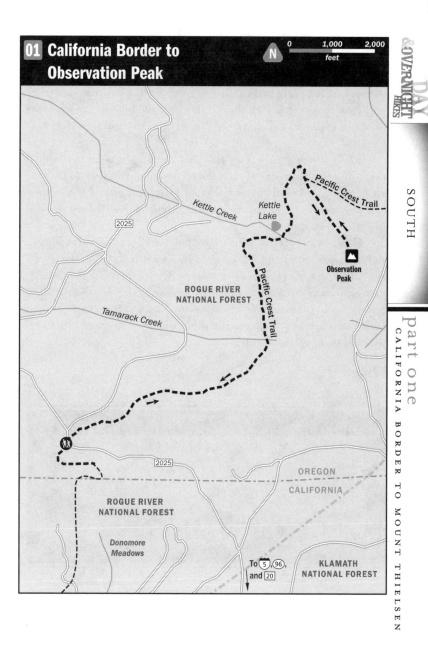

01 California Border to Observation Peak

SOUTH

part one
CALIFORNIA BORDER TO MOUNT THIELSEN

&OVERNIGHT HIKES
DAY

0   1,000   2,000
feet

N

Pacific Crest Trail

Kettle Creek

Kettle Lake

2025

Pacific Crest Trail

ROGUE RIVER
NATIONAL FOREST

Observation
Peak

Tamarack Creek

2025

OREGON

CALIFORNIA

ROGUE RIVER
NATIONAL FOREST

Donomore
Meadows

To 5, 96,
and 20

KLAMATH
NATIONAL FOREST

he had signed this register on August 4. That's about 700 miles in 26 days, or about 27 miles a day!

Now sufficiently humbled, trek back up to the road and cross it, then start a long, gradual climb along a ridge that was clear-cut years ago. Now it's covered with chaparral, whose red blooms are a favorite of hummingbirds. Up ahead you can see our destination, Observation Peak.

When you've gone 2.3 miles, you'll come upon a sunny ridge that is the west shoulder of the peak. From here, you'll be in the forest for a bit, and even cross a few small springs. It gets a little steeper at times, but it's never anything severe. Look for Kettle Lake down the hill to your left.

Half a mile past that little ridge, pop back into the open, with views to your left of rolling, forested hills stretching off to the horizon. Next, at a big rock pile, encounter the northern ridge of our peak, with fine views out toward Dutchman's Peak and its lookout. According to the book *Oregon Geographical Names*, this peak got its name from the death by freezing in the 1870s of a miner named Hensley ... who was German. Go figure.

ELEVATION PROFILE

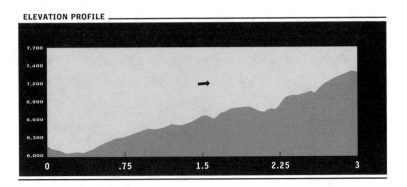

The trail now swings southeast and starts a traverse of the north side of Observation Peak, but you step off the trail just before it disappears into the woods, which are often filled with snow well into July. A short climb of 50 feet will put you on the ridgeline, which you then follow cross-country past several false summits to the real one, which is marked by a pile of rocks with a wood stake in it.

From the broad and grassy summit, which is just over 7,300 feet in elevation, you can make out FS 20 heading east toward Interstate 5 (the PCT stays very close to it all the way there), and off to the northeast, Mount McLoughlin. More to the east is Pilot Rock, the next big attraction on the PCT north and a chapter in this book. Looking south, you'll see Mount Shasta, with the Marble Mountains to its right. And finally, in a red can among the rocks, there's a summit register with entries going back to October 20, 1992! The can was also, when I opened it in September 2006, filled with hundreds of ladybugs.

A mildly interesting note about this summit is that it has two benchmarks labeled USC&GS, which stands for U.S. Coast and Geodetic Survey, a government agency that was founded in 1807 by Thomas Jefferson but hasn't existed under that name since 1970.

You can cut some distance off your return trip by going cross-country to the west; you can't miss the trail down there, but it's steep going and brushy in spots, so not recommended.

DIRECTIONS: The most direct route to this trailhead starts in the town of Jacksonville. From there, take OR 238 southwest for 7 miles to Ruch, then take Upper Applegate Rd. south for 9 miles to unpaved FS 20, which branches left (east). Follow FS 20 for 14.5 miles to Silver Fork Gap and turn southeast (downhill) on FS 2025, which is signed for Donomore Meadows. From there, it's 4.1 miles to the saddle where the PCT crosses. You can also access this area from I-5 to the east, which would make sense only if you were already in the Mount Ashland area and/or doing our Pilot Rock or Siskiyou Peak hikes. From I-5, follow FS 20 (the Mount Ashland Rd.) for 27 miles to Silver Fork Gap. Only the first 9 of these miles are paved, and some of the miles west of Meridian Overlook are quite rough.

GPS Trailhead Coordinates:	I CALIFORNIA BORDER TO OBSERVATION PEAK
UTM zone (WGS84):	10T
Easting:	507280
Northing:	465031
Latitude:	42°0.292'N
Longitude:	122°54.725'W

2 Grouse Gap *to Siskiyou Peak*

SCENERY: ⛺ ⛺ ⛺ ⛺	DISTANCE: *5.2 miles round-trip*
TRAIL CONDITION: ⛺ ⛺ ⛺	HIKING TIME: *2.5 hours*
CHILDREN: ⛺ ⛺ ⛺ ⛺	OUTSTANDING FEATURES: *A shelter to camp*
DIFFICULTY: ⛺ ⛺ ⛺	*or picnic in, interesting forest, flower-filled bowls,*
SOLITUDE: ⛺ ⛺ ⛺ ⛺	*and a wide, open mountain viewpoint*

Take a stroll up to, and then along, the spine of the Siskiyou Mountains, from a big shelter to one of the range's highest peaks. You'll see big trees, interesting rock formations, wildflowers galore, and a view that covers miles and miles.

🥾🥾 This Siskiyou section of the PCT does something fairly interesting: it runs generally east and west. This might seem odd for a trail that goes from Mexico to Canada. The reason it does so is because if the trail were to go due north from the Mount Shasta area of northern California to the area around Pilot Rock, east of here, it would go for many dry, difficult miles. In fact, before the trail was officially completed, this latter path was the route hikers took. To avoid this, the trail was built in the 1970s to swing way to the west in California, cross into Oregon, and here swing way to the east, following the spine of the Siskiyous.

That's why, when you start walking "south" on the PCT from Grouse Gap, you're actually walking to the west, and not far "north" of you, the trail swings back to the southeast. Whichever way you're headed, start by walking down the road to the Grouse Gap shelter, which is especially popular with winter recreationists who follow FS 20 into the mountains. At the shelter, you'll find a restroom, picnic tables, a huge fire pit, and a fence to keep the cows out. You can also camp here, as many PCT hikers do. I spent a night in the shelter once and heard coyotes howling and two owls hooting at each other.

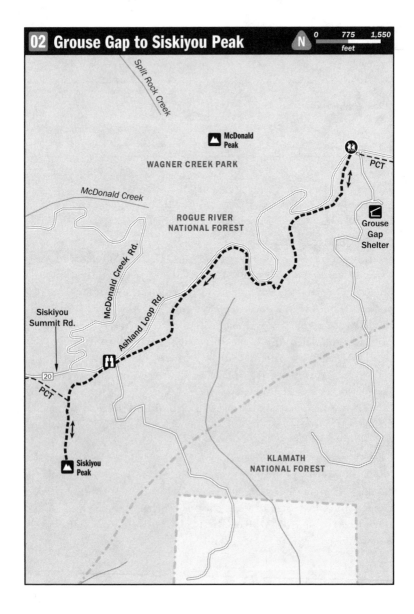

N

0   775   1,550
feet

Split Rock Creek

McDonald Peak

WAGNER CREEK PARK

PCT

McDonald Creek

ROGUE RIVER
NATIONAL FOREST

Grouse
Gap
Shelter

McDonald Creek Rd.

Siskiyou
Summit Rd.

Ashland Loop Rd.

20

PCT

Siskiyou
Peak

KLAMATH
NATIONAL FOREST

Back at the road, look for the PCT headed west and uphill, just on the south side of FS 20. Start in the open for 0.2 miles, then climb into an impressive hemlock forest filled with snags and blowdowns, many of them covered with an intensely bright green moss. The rocky ridge up ahead of you is our next destination.

Just under a mile out, you'll reach a section of forest that's interesting because there's nothing else growing in it; it's just bare, sandy ground and trees. As you get up toward the ridge, look left for Mount Ashland with its big white ball on the summit. Below it and to the right, look for Pilot Rock, which the PCT visits in another chapter of this book. At 0.9 miles, the trail gets steeper and makes a switchback to the right, with interesting rock formations above you marking the ridgetop.

When you reach the saddle, you'll see the trail ahead of you, traversing the top of a large bowl, which, in summer and early fall, is filled with flowers. Also visible are two humps on the ridge; the one on the left is Siskiyou Peak. You'll also see that you're essentially back at FS 20, and in fact if you walk up to it, you'll get a view all the way to Mount Thielsen, some 80 miles northeast as the crow flies—and about 150 PCT miles.

Drop over the ridge into the south-facing bowl and start gradually downhill, now going west. Toward the far end of the bowl,

ELEVATION PROFILE

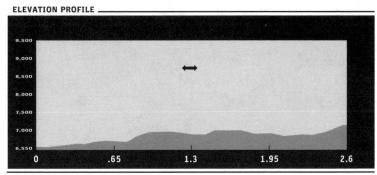

you'll almost touch FS 20 again, just below a parking area called the Meridian Overlook because it's near the Willamette Meridian. The Meridian is a line that runs north-south from a reference point located in Willamette Stone State Heritage Site on Skyline Boulevard in northwest Portland. Basically, they had to start all the surveying somewhere, and the Willamette Stone was where the surveying in the Pacific Northwest started. So, at this point, you're standing due south of northwest Portland—for whatever that's worth.

A third of a mile southwest of the overlook, when the PCT reaches a saddle just north of Siskiyou Peak, leave it and head cross-country to the summit. It's a little steep (400 feet in 0.3 miles) and, since you're heading over 7,000 feet elevation, you may get winded. But the view from the top is worth it, and there's even a summit register for you to sign. This is an excellent place to watch a sunset, by the way, especially if you have a car at the Meridian Overlook.

DIRECTIONS: From Ashland, go 12 miles south on I-5 and take Exit 6/Mount Ashland. This puts you on OR 99, which you follow south for 1 mile, still following signs for Mount Ashland. Turn right (west) onto paved Mount Ashland Rd., which turns into FS 20. In 9 miles, you'll reach the Mount Ashland Ski Area and 0.2 miles later leave the pavement. Stay right at a junction in 0.1 mile, and 2.4 miles later you'll reach Grouse Gap. Park here, on the right side of the road, or turn left and go 0.3 miles to Grouse Gap Shelter, where there's more parking and a restroom.

GPS Trailhead Coordinates	2 GROUSE GAP TO SISKIYOU PEAK
UTM zone (WGS84):	10T
Easting:	521552
Northing:	4658886
Latitude:	42°4.905'N
Longitude:	122°44.366'W

3 OR 99 *to Pilot Rock*

SCENERY: ✿ ✿ ✿	DISTANCE: *9.2 miles round-trip*
TRAIL CONDITION: ✿ ✿ ✿	HIKING TIME: *5 hours*
CHILDREN: ✿ ✿ ✿	OUTSTANDING FEATURES: *Rolling hills, open*
DIFFICULTY: ✿ ✿	*grasslands, wildflowers, wide views, solitude, and*
SOLITUDE: ✿ ✿ ✿ ✿	*some optional rock climbing*

Take a little trip through cowboy country—literally. This hike wanders through former logging and grazing lands now being restored to their natural state. You'll get some nice viewpoints that stretch into California, and you can visit a southern Oregon landmark.

🏃🏃 Among PCT hikers, this section of the trail is, shall we say, widely disrespected. The quasi-official guidebook for thru-hikers calls it "the driest, least scenic section" in Oregon and Washington, adding that it "will certainly be shunned by many" other than "long-distance hikers passing through to a more scenic destination."

Heed not such discouraging words. I happen to like the walk up to Pilot Rock for its unique character, rolling-hills cowboy feel, and solitude. And if you feel like doing a little climbing, there's a nice view as well.

If you want to skip the bulk of this hike, it's possible to drive to within a mile of Pilot Rock's summit. My directions below are to the lower trailhead. To reach the upper trailhead (which you will also hike to by following this chapter, making a shuttle possible), drive 0.6 miles past the lower trailhead on OR 99 and turn left (east) on Pilot Rock Road. This bumpy track will lead you 2 miles to a big turnout area, from which you need to stay uphill on the second road from the left. It's another bumpy mile up to the trailhead at the end of the road.

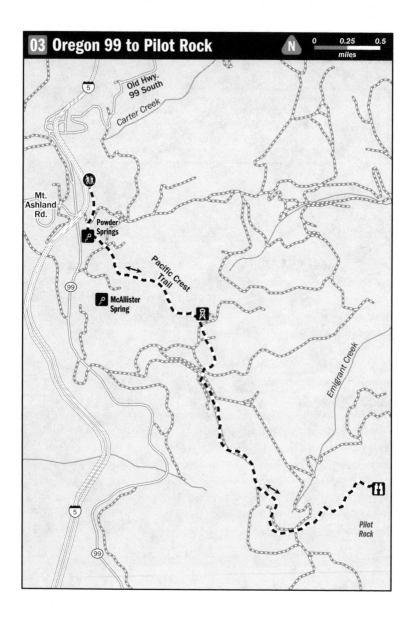

N

0   0.25   0.5

miles

Old Hwy.
99 South

Carter Creek

5

Mt.
Ashland
Rd.

Powder
Springs

Pacific Crest
Trail

McAllister
Spring

99

Emigrant Creek

5

99

Pilot
Rock

But let's do the whole walk instead. Starting from your trailhead on OR 99, you'll dip down briefly to cross a gully, then wind your way up through open grasslands. Cross over a little creek (probably dry by late summer) at 0.3 miles, and you will see the first of many signs encouraging you to stay out of the Sky King Cole Ranch and its habitat-restoration area.

This 1,300-acre parcel was purchased by a local couple in 1991 from a timber company that logged it but didn't replant it. The couple embarked on a plan to restore it, and in 2006 it was added to the 53,000-acre Cascade–Siskiyou National Monument. This was the first monument in the nation created in recognition of an area's biological diversity. The Sky King Cole property alone is said to include four separate eco-regions, 200 species of birds, and 100 species of butterflies. Its ridge separates the watersheds of the Klamath and Rogue rivers.

Just under half a mile out, drop down and around to the northeast, then cross another creek bed. This is a good time to mention that this is one of the first PCT sections in this book to become snow-free; in June and July there will be plenty of water here, as well as flowers and mosquitoes.

About 0.6 miles out, cross a footbridge and an old road, then climb to the south. Look for views of Mount Ashland across

ELEVATION PROFILE

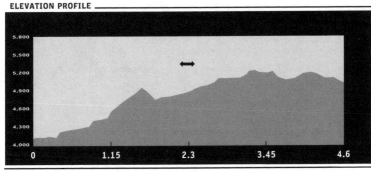

Interstate 5, and also (just past a boardwalk at 0.8 miles) a tremendous tree on your right, with a swooping canopy that touches the ground below you to the left.

After 1.4 miles, switchback to the left at a piece of metal pipe in the ground, and begin a gradual climb to the east that tops out in a flat meadow. A few minutes later, you'll pass through a gate with a Bureau of Land Management sign (be sure to close the gate behind you) and see a communication tower just ahead. If that's not appealing to you, look right for more nice views back to the Siskiyou Range and Mount Ashland.

Round the top of a ridge at 1.8 miles, cross over a little piece of boardwalk that seems to serve no purpose whatsoever, then commence another flat section bending to the west with a nice view north. We're heading for the end of that ridge you see. In this section, right at 2 miles, there's a turn that could be easy to miss. Look for a stump on your left with four trail markers and, just past that, a stake marking a left turn.

Stroll downhill now, gaining your first view of Pilot Rock. You're walking almost due south, even though you're technically northbound on the PCT. That's because the trail here is coming out of a long eastward swing through the Siskiyous. The final turn north, for Canada, is just before the upper trailhead on this hike.

At 2.2 miles, you'll come to an intersection where the trail descends just east of a road, then enjoy a nice ridgetop walk to another, major road crossing. The trail continues across the main road and between two others headed south, then it climbs gradually to a long, open ridge with views of ever-closer Pilot Rock. After a mile and a half of this, you'll drop down to yet another road, this time at the upper trailhead parking area.

Continue across the lot on the PCT, which is now very wide due to all the folks coming up to climb Pilot Rock. In 0.2 miles, you'll have a decision to make: if you want to climb the rock itself, take the wider trail heading up and to the right. I have not done this route, since every time I've been up here the weather has been unpleasant, so I can't comment on it directly. However, I've been told by other hikers and a Forest Service ranger that it's straightforward, hands-and-feet rock scrambling that doesn't require a rope.

The PCT stays left of the summit trail and in 100 yards arrives at at one of these wonderful wooden backpack rests. In 2006, this one had a journal in it with fun thru-hiker comments. Next, pass several interesting rock formations, one of which has a view left to Mount McLoughlin.

Finally, a total of 4.6 miles out, you'll come to a fine viewpoint on a shoulder of Pilot Rock's ridge. Mount Shasta is off to the south, Pilot Rock looms to your right, and there's a volcanic plug on the trail right in front of you. Volcanic or not, it makes a fine place to sit down, have a snack, and take it all in.

DIRECTIONS: From Ashland, go south on I-5 for 12 miles and take Exit 6/Mount Ashland. This puts you on OR 99, which you follow south for 1.4 miles to a gravel parking area on the left shoulder. There's no official sign here, but in various years the spot has been marked by a ribbon on a tree, a rock cairn, and a makeshift PCT sign. (See text for a shorter option.)

GPS Trailhead Coordinates	3 OR 99 TO PILOT ROCK
UTM zone (WGS84):	10T
Easting:	532991
Northing:	4657348
Latitude:	42°4.050'N
Longitude:	122°36.073'W

4 Sky Lakes Wilderness

SCENERY: ✿ ✿ ✿ ✿	DISTANCE: *20.6 miles*
TRAIL CONDITION: ✿ ✿ ✿	HIKING TIME: *2 days*
CHILDREN: ✿ ✿	OUTSTANDING FEATURES: *A series of high-*
DIFFICULTY: ✿ ✿ ✿	*altitude lakes, mountain views, and a dramatic ridge-*
SOLITUDE: ✿ ✿	*line walk*

Officially, the Pacific Crest Trail skips the best parts of Sky Lakes Wilderness. To limit impact on the lakes, it runs along a high ridge that this hike visits. But most people skip that part and visit the lakes, which is the real point here. And if you want to go up to the ridge, we'll do that, too. Warning: Do not go to the Sky Lakes in July or early August. The mosquitoes will absolutely ruin your trip. Trust me, I know.

🚶🚶 Several trails access this part of the woods, so what I am suggesting here is a loop with a car shuttle. That's because the Cherry Creek Trailhead is the easiest to get to (and arrives in the middle of the action), and the Nannie Creek Trailhead offers the easiest hike in or out—though it arrives the farthest from the good stuff. If you have only one car, start at Nannie Creek.

With the disclaimers aside, let's go for a hike, starting at Cherry Creek Trailhead. From here, the Cherry Creek Trail descends slightly through a young forest, and after a quarter mile you will hear the creek itself, off to your right. You'll see the wide, shallow creek for the first time at 0.6 miles, and soon after cross into Sky Lakes Wilderness. I mention these mileages, in part, because there are no mileages on any of the signs around here—on the rare occasion when there are signs.

At 1.5 miles, emerge into a meadowy area atop a small ridge, and at 1.7 pass an impressive boulder on the right; it looks out of place in such thick, flat woods and was probably left behind by a retreating glacier a few thousand years ago.

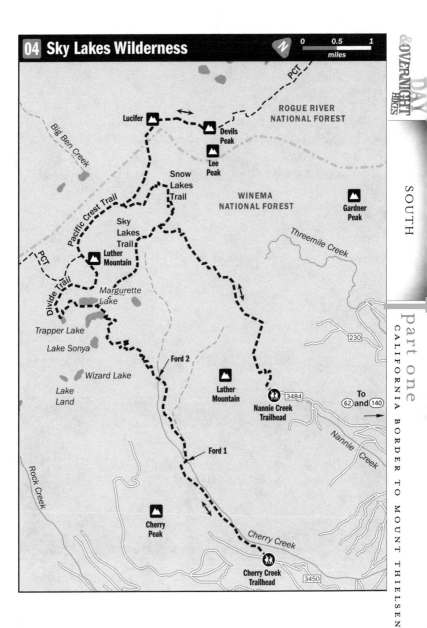

ROGUE RIVER
NATIONAL FOREST

Lucifer

Devils
Peak

Lee
Peak

Snow
Lakes
Trail

WINEMA
NATIONAL FOREST

Gardner
Peak

Pacific Crest Trail

Sky
Lakes
Trail

Luther
Mountain

Threemile Creek

Divide Trail

Margurette
Lake

Trapper Lake

Lake Sonya

Wizard Lake

Lake
Land

Ford 2

Lather
Mountain

Nannie Creek
Trailhead   3484

230

To
62 and 140

Ford 1

Nannie Creek

Rock Creek

Cherry
Peak

Cherry Creek

Cherry Creek
Trailhead   3450

You'll have to ford the creek twice on this hike, but it's no big deal either time. At 2.1 miles is a crossing with rocks to walk on, then at 3.5 is another crossing where there are often fallen logs to use. A quarter mile past that, you'll start your climb, which includes 15 well-graded switchbacks.

Just under 6 miles out, pass a small lake on your right—the first of many—as you round the last hill leading up to the much larger Trapper Lake and the Sky Lakes Trail. This is the main thoroughfare for thru-hikers skipping the PCT, which is up on the ridge you see beyond Trapper Lake. The peak up there is Luther Mountain, which is an optional scramble for later in the hike.

Turn right (north) here, and almost immediately see the Donna Lake Trail on the right. Get used to this kind of thing; there are lots of trails leading to lots of lakes up here. This one passes two lakes on its 0.9-mile course back to the Sky Lakes Trail. Skipping that, proceed around the north shore of Trapper Lake and go a quarter mile to the Divide Trail, which actually goes straight ahead.

Here's where you have a decision to make. There's camping all over the place (though some lakeshores are off-limits), but there's none up on the ridge. So if it's a 16-mile day hike you're after, go

ELEVATION PROFILE

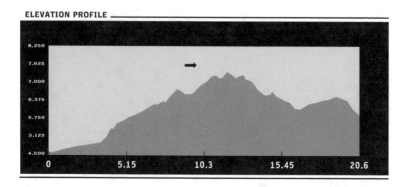

straight onto the Divide Trail. Otherwise, stay on the lower loop until you've chosen a campsite and then head up. The Divide Trail swings to the west, around the south shore of Margurette Lake, which may be the loveliest lake around. It's also off-limits to camping at its shore, though if you put in 200 yards on the Divide Trail and look for a trail heading left and uphill, you'll find a nice site on a minor ridge. There's also a fair swimming hole 300 yards down; look for a rocky point on the shoreline.

If you want to stay on the Sky Lakes Trail and skip the PCT (knocking about 4.5 miles off the hike), I'll describe that briefly: Leave Margurette Lake, passing another campsite on the right at the far (eastern) end of the lake, and walk three sections of about a half mile each, the first one flat to the far end of the Donna Lake Trail, the second one over a small hill to the lower Snow Lakes, and the third one down past Martin Lake to the Nannie Creek Trail. This is where the other loop comes down. If you were thinking about going up this way to the Upper Snow Lakes and the PCT, you should know it's *very* steep at first.

Especially if you're camping in the area, you should take the Divide Trail up to the PCT. After swinging west of Margurette Lake, the trail climbs gradually to the west, then switches back east to pass over a rocky viewing point of Margurette Lake before arriving at a series of small ponds on a ledge just south of Luther Mountain. Finally, 2.6 miles up from the Sky Lakes Trail, it intersects the PCT on a southwest spur of Luther Mountain. You can scramble a quarter mile over (and 400 feet up) to the summit for a great view of the lake-filled basin you just left behind.

Now you put in a whopping 1.3 miles of actual PCT hiking over to the Snow Lakes Trail, but there's plenty of good stuff farther north, if you're spending some time and want to explore. From this junction, which can be easy to miss because the sign tends to blow down (you'll know you missed it if you start climbing again), the PCT stays true north as it winds around the west side of Shale Butte and the east side of Lucifer before arriving, 1.7 miles later, at Devils Peak Trail (#984). This is the start of a 4.2-mile loop that swings through the Seven Lakes Basin and then comes back to the PCT, passing several large lakes on the way.

By this point, the PCT has become a serious ridge walk, with expansive views all around and, at times, big drops below. In other words, it's completely unlike any other section around and a revelation to folks hiking in from the south. From the Devils Peak Trail, the PCT makes a half-mile traverse to the real highlight of the area, the saddle between Devils Peak and Lee Peak, at 7,320 feet. Now the view stretches from Mount McLoughlin in the south to the peaks around Crater Lake, and even beyond to pointy Mount Thielsen. In PCT miles, you're looking at a distance of some 82 miles.

Heading north, as you can see, you would drop down quite a slope, which until late July will have snow on it—lots of fun with a full backpack. But there's not much to see between here and Crater Lake National Park, so you might as well head back. When you get to the Snow Lakes Trail, follow it down, and in 0.2 miles come to the Upper Snow Lakes, which are about as lovely a place to spend some time (or a night) as you can imagine. At one campsite, somebody even made some furniture out of the flat stones.

Beyond those lakes, your trail stays fairly flat for half a mile before the bottom drops out and you lose 700 feet in just over a mile down to the Nannie Creek Trail. This is also the northern end of the Sky Lakes Trail, so if you have a camp back among the lakes, that's your route home for the night; the same is true if you're doing a loop from the Cherry Creek Trailhead. If you have a car at Nannie Creek Trailhead, you've got 5 up-and-down miles to go. On the way, you'll get some nice views out into the Klamath Basin and as far south as Mount Shasta.

And for the record, I officially don't know anything about feisty, 10- to 12-inch brook trout in any of these lakes, especially the bigger ones like . . . well, as I said, I'm not reporting any such thing. You didn't hear it from me.

DIRECTIONS: Both the Cherry Creek Trailhead and Nannie Creek Trailhead are accessible from CR 531, which is also known as Westside Rd. From Klamath Falls, go 26 miles west on SR 140 and turn north onto Westside, following signs for Rocky Point. For the Cherry Creek Trailhead, go 12 miles north and turn left onto FS 3450, which leads 2 miles to the trailhead. For the Nannie Creek Trailhead, go another mile north on 531 and turn left onto FS 3484, which leads 6 miles to the trailhead.

GPS Trailhead Coordinates	4 SKY LAKES WILDERNESS: CHERRY CREEK
UTM zone (WGS84):	10T
Easting:	572486
Northing:	4715550
Latitude:	42°36.8158'N
Longitude:	122°8.8551'W

GPS Trailhead Coordinates	4 SKY LAKES WILDERNESS: NANNIE CREEK
UTM zone (WGS84):	10T
Easting:	569913
Northing:	4718259
Latitude:	42°35.3380'N
Longitude:	122°6.9937'W

5 OR 62 *to* Pumice Flats

SCENERY: ⛺ ⛺
TRAIL CONDITION: ⛺ ⛺ ⛺
CHILDREN: ⛺ ⛺ ⛺
DIFFICULTY: ⛺
SOLITUDE: ⛺ ⛺ ⛺ ⛺

DISTANCE: *Up to 15 miles*
HIKING TIME: *7 hours*
OUTSTANDING FEATURES: *Pristine hemlock forest, solitude, interesting volcanic geology*

Although this hike is in Crater Lake National Park, I've seen more elk on it than people. Short on dramatic views, it is nonetheless long on forest, peace, and quiet, and you have two options for destinations: a rocky peak and a unique volcanic landscape. Note: Pets are not allowed on this or any other trails in Crater Lake National Park.

🚶🚶 It's amazing how easy it is to leave people behind in a national park. Hundreds of people drive by this trailhead every day without even noticing it, yet two interesting hikes start from it: this one and our OR 62 to Crater Lake Rim hike. Both introduce you to the part of the park that's away from the lake and, therefore, away from the RVs, gift shops, restaurants, lines, and so on. This one, especially, is all about solitude.

From the parking lot, head south on the PCT, and in just a couple of minutes you'll encounter an interesting forest feature: a small area that was cut years ago and is now filled with young trees, all the same species and height, and all of them leaning about 15 degrees to the right—presumably because of wind and snow. Also in this area, look for a section of tree suspended about 20 feet off the ground between two other trees; it was there in 2006 when I came through, and the rest of it was scattered all around the trail.

Forest attractions like this will dominate your view for a while as you wind through the woods without much effort. Look for other features like logs that were cut to clear for trail (exposing their growth

05 Oregon 62 to Pumice Flats

DAY
&OVERNIGHT
HIKES

SOUTH

part one
CALIFORNIA BORDER TO MOUNT THIELSEN

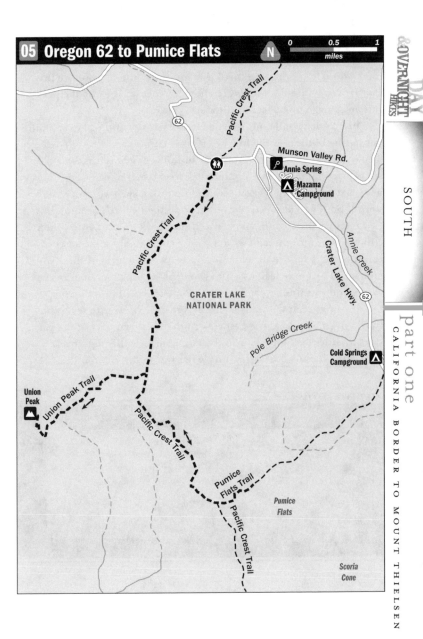

N

0   0.5   1
miles

Pacific Crest Trail

62

Munson Valley Rd.

Annie Spring

Mazama
Campground

Annie Creek

Crater Lake Hwy.

Pacific Crest Trail

CRATER LAKE
NATIONAL PARK

Pole Bridge Creek

62

Cold Springs
Campground

Union
Peak

Union Peak Trail

Pacific Crest Trail

Pacific Crest Trail

Pumice
Flats Trail

Pumice
Flats

Pacific Crest Trail

Scoria
Cone

rings), rotting snags, the spiral pattern of wood in dead trees, and woodpecker holes in bark. Also look for blue diamonds up in the trees; those mark the trail for skiers and snowshoers, who love this easy grade. Those diamonds are about 20 feet up because the park gets an average of 44 feet of snow every year!

Just under a mile out, start downhill a little, and just over a mile out, at the bottom of the hill, see if you can spot an ancient road heading off to the right. About five minutes past this, on the right, are two spectacularly rotting snags—perfect cones of red wood. It was here that I scared up several elk, who bounded away without making a sound. So if you also can stay quiet, you might get to see some as well.

Around the 2-mile mark, you'll start back uphill a little, then climb a little more steeply as you swing to the right (southwest) in a forest of huge mountain hemlocks—among the largest of these you'll ever see. The grade lessens a bit as you pass through a notch in the ridge, and just under 3 miles you'll come to a trail junction.

If you're feeling up for a climb, stay straight here to leave the PCT for Union Peak, the best view in the southern part of the park. It's 2.6 miles to the peak. You'll climb gradually through forest for the first 0.8 miles, then stay mostly flat for another 0.8 miles,

ELEVATION PROFILE

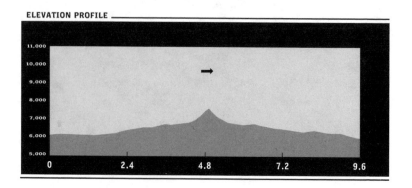

traversing the south side of the peak and passing in and out of the woods. The trail then turns north, starts a series of switchbacks, and becomes quite steep and rocky; the last 0.6 miles gain a whopping 700 feet, and at times you'll find yourself using hands and feet to make progress. This route is shown on our elevation profile, bracketed by the Union Peak Trail Junction.

If that doesn't sound like quite your bag, stay left and on the PCT at the junction, following a sign for Stuart Falls. The PCT climbs again after leaving the Union Peak Trail then swings left (southeast) for a flat, forested stretch. Crater Peak, visible a few miles away to your left, is another hiking destination in the park. It's across a pumice flat smaller than the one you're headed for, and if you wanted to head off cross-country to this one, just make sure you know how to get back!

In this meandering, mostly flat stretch, look for a big gray snag with a tremendous burl eight feet off the ground, as well as a clump of eight or nine hemlocks bunched together on the left. There's also a view of craggy Union Peak to the right. Finally, 2.1 miles after the Union Peak junction, reach the Stuart Falls Trail heading south; this 50-foot plunge is worth a visit and has a campsite at its base, but at 2.5 miles from here, it makes a long day, so consider coming at it from other trailheads outside the park, or from the park's Lodgepole Picnic Area (see below). There's also great camping at Stuart Falls.

Stay on the PCT for just a few more minutes to reach a junction with the Pumice Flats Trail and its PCT register. It's fun to read these remarks, especially from the northbounders, who typically arrive in mid-August with dreams of showers and beer and dinner at the Crater Lake Lodge filling their heads. The Pumice Flats Trail, actually an abandoned road, drops down for about half a mile onto the flats, which are filled with lodgepole pine and (according to park rangers) elk. These pumice flats are essentially valleys that were filled with volcanic spew when Mount Mazama erupted thousands of years ago.

The Pumice Flats Trail keeps going another 2.3 miles to a trailhead on OR 62 near the Lodgepole Picnic Area, so it's possible to do this hike as a one-way shuttle with a second car there. Lodgepole is 3.5 miles south on OR 62 from the trailhead parking area described in the beginning of this hike.

DIRECTIONS: From Medford, take OR 62 east for 75 miles to the PCT parking area on the right. This lot is 0.8 miles west of the south entrance to Crater Lake National Park, so there's no fee or permit required to hike this trail, even though it is in the park.

GPS Trailhead Coordinates	5 OR 62 TO PUMICE FLATS
UTM zone (WGS84):	10T
Easting:	566971
Northing:	4746837
Latitude:	42°52.272'N
Longitude:	122°10.804'W

6 OR 62 *to* Crater Lake Rim

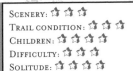

SCENERY: ✿ ✿ ✿	DISTANCE: *4.3 miles one way*
TRAIL CONDITION: ✿ ✿ ✿	HIKING TIME: *2.5 hours*
CHILDREN: ✿ ✿ ✿ ✿	OUTSTANDING FEATURES: *Quiet forest, a*
DIFFICULTY: ✿ ✿ ✿	*lovely creek, excellent campsites, and a sturdy climb*
SOLITUDE: ✿ ✿ ✿ ✿	*that makes a great view even better*

How do you make the view of Crater Lake even better? The old-fashioned way: you earn it! Walk up there instead of driving, or just use this seldom-visited piece of PCT to explore the woods, enjoy some wildflowers, or add a secluded overnight backpack to your park visit. Note: No pets are allowed on this or any other trail in Crater Lake National Park.

🚶🚶 From this section's founding in 1973, the PCT, incredibly, avoided the rim of Crater Lake. This was because horses were (and are) allowed on the trail, but not up at the rim. To this day, if you were to hike the official PCT across Crater Lake National Park, you'd never lay your eyes on the lake—or much else, for that matter.

But from the beginning, owing to simple common sense, hikers took off up the Dutton Creek Trail to the rim, then made their way along the Rim Drive and the north access road, following them back to the PCT. Finally, in the 1990s, the Park Service relented and built a route along the rim called a "hiker's PCT," since horses are still not allowed up there. That hike is described in our Crater Lake Rim chapter, and this one is a taste of the original trail.

You can do just the first half of this hike and not put in much effort at all, reaching a lovely creek in flower-filled meadows with excellent camping nearby—an excellent hike to take the kids on. Or you can do the whole thing and climb 1,000 feet in 2 miles to wind up at the rim. Or start at the top and walk down to the creek—suit yourself!

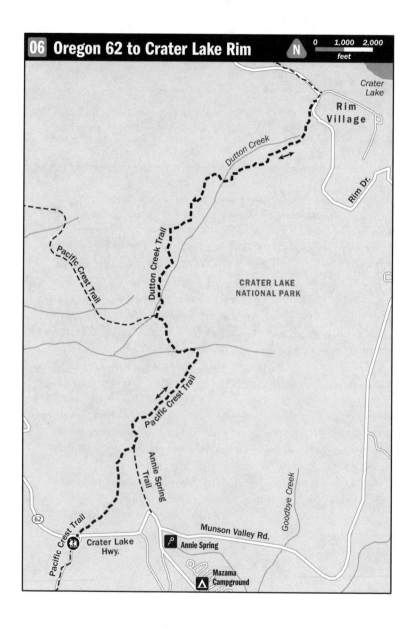

N

0   1,000   2,000
feet

Crater
Lake

**Rim
Village**

Dutton Creek

Rim Dr.

Dutton Creek Trail

**CRATER LAKE
NATIONAL PARK**

Pacific Crest Trail

Pacific Crest Trail

Pacific Crest Trail

Annie Spring Trail

Goodbye Creek

62

Munson Valley Rd.

Pacific Crest Trail

Crater Lake
Hwy.

Annie Spring

**Mazama
Campground**

From the trailhead on OR 62, walk to and then across the highway, tending slightly to your right and looking for the trail reentering the woods on the north side of the road; you might spot a white or blue diamond on a tree, or perhaps a rock cairn along the road. The trail starts out flat through trees and meadows; look for a big, impressive, hollowed-out snag on the right, at the head of a meadow about 0.2 miles in. Even if it's mid-August and northbound thru-hikers are on the move, you probably won't see them, since most take a "zero day" over at Mazama Village's campground, store, and restaurant.

A total of 0.3 miles in, you'll start climbing a bit, and if you've just arrived in the vicinity, you might feel short of breath. At 6,200 feet elevation, it doesn't take much. You'll climb up the west side of a small ridge and, 0.6 miles from the road, intersect the Annie Spring Trail, which descends right to the Mazama Village.

After dropping again, wind through a grassy hemlock forest with occasional views to the left of the Watchman and Hillman peaks, up on the rim. Yes, you're going down on your way up to the rim, and don't ask me why.

When you've gone 1.7 miles, you'll cross the first of three forks of Dutton Creek at the head of a grassy meadow, which, in early

ELEVATION PROFILE

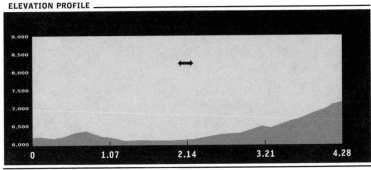

summer (July, around here) will be filled with flowers. At the second fork, 0.3 miles later, a series of stones has been placed for you to walk over. And 0.1 mile after that, just before the westernmost fork, you'll intersect the Dutton Creek Trail.

Beyond this, the PCT is just more of the same. A stake on the left marks a trail to campsites along the creek below the trail; you'll need a permit from the park to camp here, but it's a lovely area that's likely to have few, if any, visitors.

Heading up the Dutton Creek Trail now, it's nothing too fancy: just a long series of switchbacks through the forest, crossing various forks of Dutton Creek several times, with little or nothing in the way of views—until the top, of course. It's 2.2 miles to the access road, and for your reference, when you actually drop down briefly (again!) to a creek crossing, you've gone 1.3 miles and gained 400 feet; this means it's about to get steeper, as in 650 feet over the last mile.

But you'll feel oh, so cool when you get to the rim, right? You can walk tall among the RV-driving picture takers, knowing that you had the strength to *walk* to the rim of Crater Lake!

DIRECTIONS: From Medford, take OR 62 east for 75 miles to the PCT parking area on the right. This lot is 0.8 miles west of the south entrance to Crater Lake National Park, so there's no fee or permit required to hike this trail, even though it is in the park.

GPS Trailhead Coordinates	6 OR 62 TO CRATER LAKE RIM
UTM zone (WGS84):	10T
Easting:	566971
Northing:	4746837
Latitude:	42°52.272'N
Longitude:	122°10.804'W

7 Crater Lake Rim

SCENERY: ☆ ☆ ☆ ☆	DISTANCE: *6.4 miles one way*
TRAIL CONDITION: ☆ ☆ ☆	HIKING TIME: *3 hours*
CHILDREN: ☆ ☆ ☆	OUTSTANDING FEATURES: *A 6-mile-wide,*
DIFFICULTY: ☆ ☆	*1,900-foot-deep lake, 1,000 feet below you, with*
SOLITUDE: ☆	*mountains all around. Need anything else?*

This bit of trail is so amazing that it has become part of the PCT. So many people were walking off the original trail to see Oregon's most stupendous site that the Park Service built this section of trail as a "hiker's PCT." And you'll see why, as you meander along the rim of the caldera, enjoying view after view after view. Note: Pets are not allowed on trails in Crater Lake National Park, and they must be leashed elsewhere in the park.

🚶🚶 As the PCT winds its way across Oregon, it passes in and out of amazing scenery—none more amazing than Crater Lake. It also passes through solitary areas and crowded ones—none more crowded than Crater Lake. Still, this easy walk is the best way to experience the Crater Lake Rim, because 99 percent of the throngs will stick to the road and parking areas, while you're hiking from one private viewing area to the next.

Before the 1990s, when the PCT still stayed 1,000 feet below the rim, hikers would walk up the Dutton Creek Trail to the Rim Village, then make their way along the road or off-trail to the north access road. But during the 1990s, the Park Service built the trail you're about to walk, a one-way 6-miler that parallels the road. (Horses must stick to the official PCT.) On this trail, you can do as little as you want, or you can use a second car to do a shuttle, or you can do a 12-mile round-trip that should take no more than five hours. (The hike up the Dutton Creek Trail is described in our chapter called "OR 62 to Crater Lake Rim.")

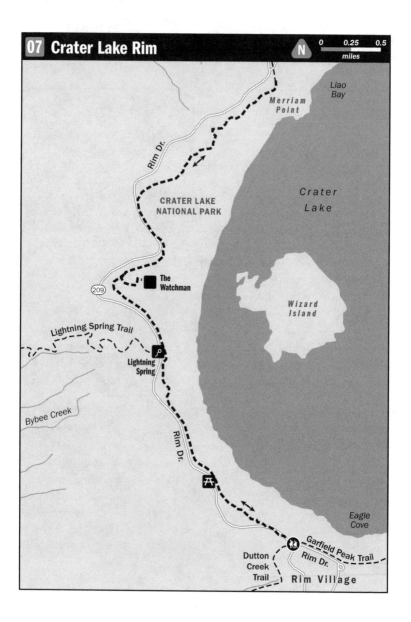

N

0   0.25   0.5
miles

Liao Bay

Merriam Point

Rim Dr.

Crater Lake

CRATER LAKE NATIONAL PARK

209

■ The Watchman

Wizard Island

Lightning Spring Trail

Lightning Spring

Bybee Creek

Rim Dr.

Eagle Cove

Garfield Peak Trail

Dutton Creek Trail

Rim Dr.

Rim Village

Starting at the Rim Village, just walk up to the rim and turn left, along a stone wall with the lake on your right. Try to wrap your head around the distances involved: it's *6 miles* to the other side of the lake, and the distance from you to the lake (about 1,000 feet in most places) is about half that from the surface to the bottom! And by the way, it's a caldera, not a crater. Mount Mazama imploded to form this, the deepest lake in the United States and the seventh deepest in the world.

When you get to the top of the access road, the trail drops down 0.1 mile to the first of many cliffs; needless to say, be real careful here. At 0.2 miles, you'll reach the first of several parking areas along the road, and the trail starts back up with views of Wizard Island, which is a lava cone that built up after the caldera was formed; you can take a highly recommended boat ride to it during the summer.

The next mile or so takes you away from the road, up a hill of a hundred feet or so, to several spots where you're even more exposed to the edge of the cliffs; this is not a hike for folks afraid of heights! At 1.1 mile, you'll be back to the road at a big parking area with outhouses. Looking south from this area, you can see Mount McLoughlin and the prominent Devils Peak, a PCT landmark described in our "Sky Lakes Loop" chapter; to the PCT hiker, that's about 22 miles away.

ELEVATION PROFILE

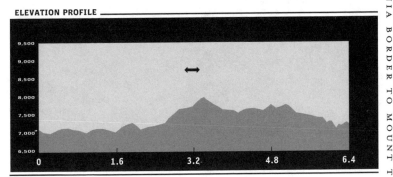

Check out some of the interpretive signs in this parking area, then head up some switchbacks and over another hill, this one reaching as high as 7,319 feet above sea level (about 200 feet above the last parking area). Looking ahead here, see The Watchman with its lookout tower; you can go there in a bit, if you'd like.

At 2.2 miles, you'll drop down a steep little pitch to the road again and have your closest view of Wizard Island. Find the trail at the far end of the parking lot, where it heads up the hill right before a sign saying "Lightning Springs 500 feet." Reach the Lightning Springs picnic area in 0.2 miles, and across the road you'll see the trailhead of the same name. This is another access trail from the official PCT down the hill, and if you start down it, you'll come to a spring and campground in 0.8 miles. You'll need a permit from the park to camp here.

From the Lightning Springs picnic area, the trail bends out to the west to get around The Watchman. It also climbs steadily, gaining 500 feet in 0.7 miles to a junction with the trail to The Watchman's summit. Since you're up here, go on up to the summit, which is 0.4 miles and 300 feet above you; it's a well-graded climb to the peak at 8,013 feet. The views stretch from California's Mount Shasta north to the Three Sisters, just sticking up to the left of needle-pointed Mount Thielsen. And the lake, of course.

There are two stories about how The Watchman got its name: In 1886, a group of engineers was placed here to take observations while another group toured the lake by boat, taking soundings of its depth. But before that, in 1871, three men climbed up here; one died from exertion, and while one man went for help, another watched over the body.

Back on the trail below The Watchman, traverse a boulder field before dropping down to a big parking area with more outhouses and interpretive signs. At this point, if you've gone up to The Watchman, you've hiked a total of 4.1 miles since leaving Rim Village. Pick up the trail at the far end of the lot's fences, just past the outhouse, and enjoy 1.2 miles of open strolling around the west side of Hillman Peak, the highest spot on the rim, named for one of the lake's "discoverers" in 1853. Along this stretch, you'll start to get views north to Diamond Lake, Mount Thielsen, and the Three Sisters, as well as the immense pumice flats that northbound PCT hikers have to look forward to.

At 5.9 miles, the trail empties out onto the road just around the corner from another parking area. Go 100 yards and look for where the trail resumes on a dirt mound at the far end of the lot; walk up that and aim for a clump of gnarled trees. At the next parking area, in 0.1 mile, pick up the trail at the end of a stone guardrail, just before another clump of trees.

Finally, after one last little hump, you'll come to a parking area with road signs for the Rim Drive continuing east. At this point, you're done. The trail crosses the Rim Drive just east of the North Access Road, then heads north from a rock cairn for 11.5 miles of viewless, waterless, pumice-filled joy to OR 138. Hikers who started at the Rim Village have to walk your 6 miles, those 11.5 miles, and then another 8 miles to Thielsen Creek before they cross a drop of water. Aren't you glad you aren't doing *that* with a full pack?

DIRECTIONS: From Medford, travel east on OR 62 for 76 miles to the south entrance to Crater Lake National Park. The entrance fee is $10 per vehicle and is good for 10 days. Follow the south access road 7.5 miles to Rim Village, where parking is abundant.

GPS Trailhead Coordinates	7 CRATER LAKE RIM
UTM zone (WGS84):	10T
Easting:	569562
Northing:	4751404
Latitude:	42°54.725'N
Longitude:	122°8.867'W

8 Mount Thielsen Loop

SCENERY: ☘ ☘ ☘
TRAIL CONDITION: ☘ ☘ ☘
CHILDREN: ☘
DIFFICULTY: ☘ ☘ ☘ ☘
SOLITUDE: ☘ ☘ ☘

DISTANCE: *16.9 miles*
HIKING TIME: *2 days*
OUTSTANDING FEATURES: *Staggering views from a peak over 9,000 feet, high-elevation forest, and camping by a tumbling mountain stream*

Even if you aren't into mountain climbing and don't want to tackle "The Lightning Rod of the Cascades," this hike is worth the effort for big views and a chance to camp way up in the hills. Only about 4 of these 17 miles are on the PCT, but they are not your average 4 miles.

👫 This hike starts out with one of the most fantastically confusing trail signs you're likely to see. It's one thing when signs have the wrong distances or something, but this one seems designed to make you stop and scratch your head. You've got Trail 1448, a "connection" to Trail 1448, and then, 4 miles ahead, Trail 1448. Huh?

Don't worry about it; just turn left and follow Trail 1448, the Howlock Mountain Trail. It passes under the highway at 0.2 miles, then a mile later reaches Trail 1458, the Spruce Ridge Trail. Turn right here and climb gradually for another 0.7 miles before things flatten out for 2 miles over to Trail 1456, the Mount Thielsen Trail. Turn left here as well, and now you'll start climbing. You'll also get a nice view of Mount Thielsen just after starting up.

After 2.6 miles and 1,300 feet, arrive at the PCT on a narrow, western ridge of Thielsen. This is where you have a decision to make. To simply continue your loop on the PCT (and reach creekside campsites in 2.3 miles), turn left here. If you want to climb the peak, follow the climber's path straight up. Note: I have not climbed Mount Thielsen, because I have a knack for showing up for this hike in horrible weather (three times, three snowstorms!). But I have distilled the

54

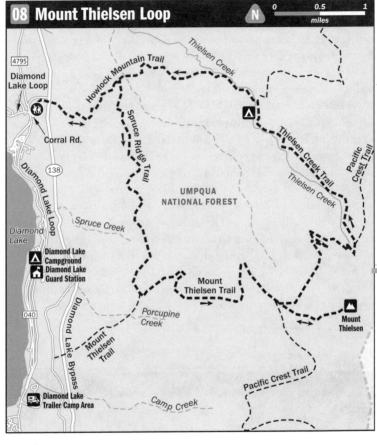

08 Mount Thielsen Loop

N

0   0.5   1
miles

Thielsen Creek

Howlock Mountain Trail

4795
Diamond Lake Loop

Corral Rd.

Spruce Ridge Trail

Thielsen Creek Trail

Pacific Crest Trail

Thielsen Creek

138

Diamond Lake Loop

UMPQUA NATIONAL FOREST

Spruce Creek

Diamond Lake

Diamond Lake Campground
Diamond Lake Guard Station

040

Mount Thielsen Trail

Porcupine Creek

Mount Thielsen Trail

Mount Thielsen

Diamond Lake Bypass

Diamond Lake Trailer Camp Area

Camp Creek

Pacific Crest Trail

following suggestions for the climb, which does not require ropes (though a helmet and stiff-soled boots are highly recommended): emerging from the trees, the trail ascends steeply over loose rock, following the south side of the mountain's west ridge. The 80-foot summit block is definitely a rock climb, so there's no shame in not tackling it. If you do, the route is up the south side; as you come up, look for a notch leading around to that side. Coming down, people take a slightly different route (going down a scree slope that isn't worth coming up). From the base of the summit block, hike south a short way down the ridge to a spot near pinnacles on the east side, then follow an obvious trail down the scree slope to the trail.

Meanwhile, back on the PCT, the trip north from the junction with the climber's trail is loaded with views, especially of the dramatic west side of Thielsen. The trail continues for a mile to the northwest ridge, from which you get a view north to Diamond Peak, the next destination on the PCT (some 42 hiker miles away).

Now the trail switches back a few times, generally tracking east across a bowl that is almost guaranteed to hold some snow well into July. If you lose the trail, just do a slightly descending eastward trek, aiming for Thielsen Creek about 400 feet lower than the ridge you just came around. Just beyond that spot, the trail starts back to the west and, in 0.1 mile, intersects Thielsen Creek Trail (#1449). A hundred yards down this is a side trail to Thielsen Camp. Consider camping here as many thru-hikers do. (They'll be here in mid- to

ELEVATION PROFILE

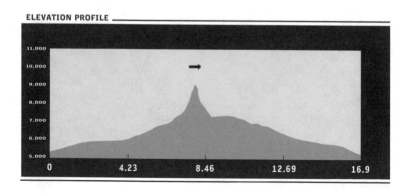

late August.) This creek is the only year-round water on the trail for 21 miles south and 33 miles north!

If you're looking to extend this trip, or connect it with the Tipsoo Peak and Maidu Lake chapter, keep going north on the PCT; you'll intersect the Howlock Mountain Trail in 3.1 miles. Otherwise, spend the night here and descend the Thielsen Creek Trail, which follows the creek for 2.1 miles to its intersection with Howlock Mountain Trail. Turn left here, and you're 3.5 miles from the car.

DIRECTIONS: The Howlock Mountain Trailhead lies just off OR 138, 4.2 miles north of its intersection with OR 230. That intersection is 79 miles east of Roseburg on 138 and 82 miles east of Medford on 230. Traveling north on 138, look for a sign that says Diamond Lake Recreation Area and FS 4795. The trailhead is 0.3 miles down that road on the left; it shares a parking lot with the Diamond Lake Corrals. A Northwest Forest Pass is required.

GPS Trailhead Coordinates	8 MOUNT THIELSEN LOOP
UTM zone (WGS84):	10T
Easting:	570422
Northing:	4781577
Latitude:	43°11.021'N
Longitude:	122°8.006'W

9 Tipsoo Peak *and* Maidu Lake

SCENERY: ☆ ☆ ☆ ☆	DISTANCE: *30.4 miles*
TRAIL CONDITION: ☆ ☆ ☆	HIKING TIME: *2 days*
CHILDREN: ☆	OUTSTANDING FEATURES: *Mountain streams,*
DIFFICULTY: ☆ ☆ ☆ ☆	*panoramic views, camping by a beautiful lake*
SOLITUDE: ☆ ☆ ☆ ☆	

Don't be scared off by the length of this one. Think of it as three possible hikes in one: either a moderate climb to camping at Thielsen Creek (about 7 miles), a strenuous trek to Tipsoo Peak's amazing views (17 miles) or a long two- or three-day excursion to Maidu Lake. This can also be combined with the Mount Thielsen Loop for a real multiday adventure. And for what it's worth, this hike visits the highest point on the Oregon–Washington PCT.

🚶🚶 This hike will take you from one of the more populated areas around, Diamond Lake, to one of the loneliest, highest, and driest stretches of Oregon's Pacific Crest Trail. In fact, one reason the suggested hike here is so long is that once you get to the PCT, there's neither water nor camping to be found for several miles either way. But the views and the solitude more than make up for the length and hassle.

Things are somewhat confusing at the trailhead, because there seem to be multiple trails going the same way, and in fact there are. What you're after is Trail 1448, the Howlock Mountain Trail, which after a quarter mile passes under OR 138. Stay with #1448 for another mile to an intersection with Trail 1458, the Spruce Ridge Trail. This trail heads right (southeast) from here and is the beginning of the Mount Thielsen Loop. For Tipsoo Peak, stay straight on #1448 and in 0.1 mile cross a seasonal fork of Thielsen Creek.

The steepness lets up over the next mile, which brings you to Timothy Meadows and the main stem of Thielsen Creek. You'll walk

N

0   1   2
miles

DESCHUTES
NATIONAL
FOREST

PCT

North Umpqua Trail

Pacific Crest Trail

Red Cinder
Butte

Thirsty Creek

Maidu
Lake

Cinnamon
Butte

UMPQUA
NATIONAL FOREST

Pacific Crest Trail

Tipsoo
Peak

Tipsoo Creek

Red
Cone

Pacific Crest Trail

Howlock Creek

(138)

Thielsen Creek

WINEMA
NATIONAL
FOREST

Pacific Crest Trail

Howlock
Mountain

1458

Diamond
Lake

Diamond Lake
Campground

Sink Creek

Diamond Lake
Guard Station

1456

Mount
Thielsen

Porcupine Creek

040

Camp Creek

Cottonwood Creek

Diamond Lake
Trailer Camp Area

Hollys
Ridge

Pacific Crest Trail

DAY
&OVERNIGHT
HIKES

SOUTH

part one
CALIFORNIA BORDER TO MOUNT THIELSEN

along the creek for almost a mile before crossing it, and you could find camping under some trees in this area, if you don't want to haul your pack the rest of the way up the hill. Just make sure you camp at least 100 feet from trails and water. This would also make a nice picnic and turnaround spot; a round-trip would be 6.8 miles with a total gain of just 800 feet.

Beyond the creek, the climb resumes for 3.6 more miles (and 1,200 feet) to the PCT. About 2 miles up, you'll round a ridge and trek back to the east, at which point 8,324-foot Howlock Mountain (named for a local Paiute chief) will dominate the view ahead.

Intersect the PCT on the edge of a pumice flat with a big-time view, from Mount Thielsen on your right to Sawtooth Ridge and Howlock Mountain in front of you. Snow lingers up here into July most years, so if you're here in early summer, there might be seasonal creeks flowing, and therefore some camping options. The whole area goes dry as soon as the snow is gone, though.

Turn left (north) onto the PCT and climb for 0.4 miles to a saddle, then traverse north through meadows and pumice where posts occasionally mark the trail. When the saddle is 1.3 miles behind you, cross over another, inconspicuous saddle that is significant for

ELEVATION PROFILE

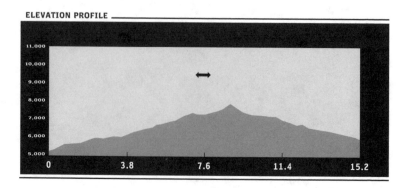

us in two ways. One, it's the turnoff point to climb reddish Tipsoo Peak to your left, and two, at 7,560 feet, it's the highest point on the PCT in Oregon and Washington.

There's no trail to Tipsoo, but it's just sitting right there. The peak on the left is the higher of the two, and the peak's left side offers the most gradual climb. It's rocky going, but the view is worth the half-hour slog. Mount Thielsen dominates to the south, with Diamond Lake visible to the right of it. To the north, it's possible to just make out (from right to left) Mount Bachelor as well as South and Middle Sister. For the northbound PCT hiker, South Sister is about 100 miles ahead.

Back down on the trail at the saddle, you can turn back (you're 8.8 miles from the trailhead and 5.4 miles from Thielsen Creek) or put in another 6 downhill miles to Maidu Lake. Along the way, you'll get views of the colorful north side of Tipsoo Peak (which, by the way, is a Chinook word for "hair") and east to Miller Lake and Red Cone. Otherwise, it's just an easy descent with not much to see.

Five miles down from the saddle, reach the Maidu Lake Trail and take it left for 0.9 miles to the lake. There's plenty of camping on the near shore, but if you happen to get there in July or early August there will also be a maddening swarm of mosquitoes. Some old maps show a shelter at this location, but it's long gone.

Maidu Lake is the headwaters of the North Umpqua River, one of the more beautiful rivers in Oregon, as well as a sought-after steelhead fishing destination. I mention this because the North Umpqua Trail starts at the lake and follows the river for 75 miles, passing campgrounds and lakes and hot springs along the way. Something to think about when you're done with your PCT adventures.

DIRECTIONS: The Howlock Mountain Trailhead lies just off OR 138, 4.2 miles north of its intersection with OR 230. That intersection is 79 miles east of Roseburg on 138 and 82 miles east of Medford on 230. Traveling north on 138, look for a sign that says Diamond Lake Recreation Area and FS 4795. The trailhead is 0.3 miles down that road on the left; it shares a parking lot with the Diamond Lake Corrals. A Northwest Forest Pass is required.

GPS Trailhead Coordinates	9 TIPSOO PEAK AND MAIDU LAKE
UTM zone (WGS84):	10T
Easting:	570422
Northing:	4781577
Latitude:	43°11.021'N
Longitude:	122°8.006'W

Central

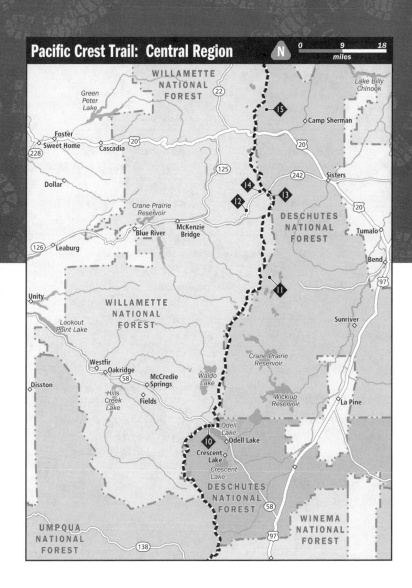

Pacific Crest Trail: Central Region

N

0   9   18
miles

10 Rosary Lakes *to* Maiden Peak Shelter

SCENERY: 🥾 🥾	DISTANCE: *6.6 miles to North Rosary Lake*
TRAIL CONDITION: 🥾 🥾 🥾 🥾	*(out-and-back); 11.6 miles to shelter (out-and-back)*
CHILDREN: 🥾 🥾 🥾 🥾	HIKING TIME: *3.5 hours*
DIFFICULTY: 🥾 🥾	OUTSTANDING FEATURES: *A quiet walk*
SOLITUDE: 🥾 🥾 🥾	*through shady forest to three mountain lakes, with a*
	nice view and hidden cabin if you want to go farther

This is an easily reached, easily hiked little leg stretcher that's perfect for an afternoon outing or a simple overnighter with the family. And if you put in a few more miles, you can spend the night in a wonderful cabin.

🥾🥾 The hike up to the Rosary Lakes is one of the more popular in the area, and it's no wonder. PCT hikers tend to blow on through, however, since most stop at Odell Lake for rest and resupply. So chances are, you'll see other folks on the trail, and chances are, you won't care.

The first 2 miles or so are about as gradual and mellow as a hike can be. There's not much to see, other than big trees and the occasional glimpse of Odell Lake off to the right, and the total trip to Lower Rosary Lake is 2.4 miles and gains just over 500 feet.

Just for reference, at 0.9 miles, the trail turns to the north in a flat section and enters a younger forest with much less ground cover. At 1.4 miles, it reenters the more diverse forest, and at 1.6 look for a gigantic hemlock snag covered with woodpecker holes. Finally, just past 1.8 miles, round the eastern edge of a minor ridge and turn north, leaving the sounds of cars and trains behind.

When you get to the first lake at 2.4 miles, look for good swimming off a rockslide to your left and campsites on a round-the-lake path. Other good campsites are along the right side of the lake, across the PCT from the shore.

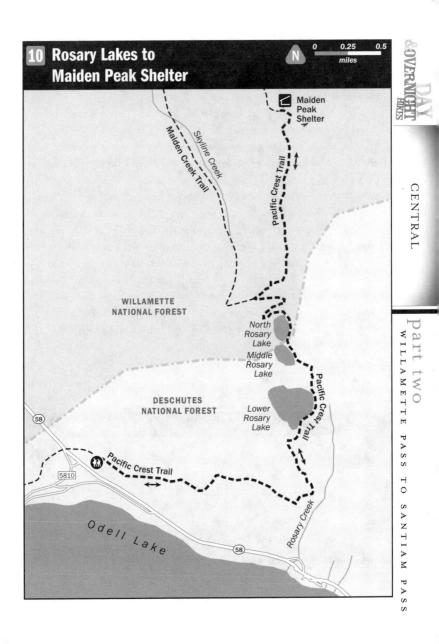

10 Rosary Lakes to Maiden Peak Shelter

0   0.25   0.5
miles

N

DAY &OVERNIGHT HIKES

CENTRAL

part two
WILLAMETTE PASS TO SANTIAM PASS

Maiden Peak Shelter

Skyline Creek

Maiden Creek Trail

Pacific Crest Trail

WILLAMETTE NATIONAL FOREST

North Rosary Lake

Middle Rosary Lake

Lower Rosary Lake

Pacific Crest Trail

DESCHUTES NATIONAL FOREST

58

Pacific Crest Trail

5810

Rosary Creek

Odell Lake

58

Past the lake, climb gently again, back in the forest, and 0.3 miles past the lower lake, arrive at Middle Rosary Lake, which is the most scenic of all. It's surprisingly deep, for the elevation, and Pulpit Rock across the way makes a handsome backdrop.

There's a fine campsite between Middle and Upper Rosary lakes, a distance of only 100 yards.

Now, if you want to get a nicer view of the lakes and possibly spend the night in some unique accommodations, put in some more mileage north on the PCT.

Continue north beyond North Rosary Lake, climbing 300 feet in a mile to Maiden Peak Saddle, with lake-filled views to the south. After a smidge more climbing, continue north along the east side of a ridge for a total of 1.6 miles; just before the PCT, cross to the west side of the ridge, and look for a cairn on the trail at the edge of an open flat. Across that flat is the Maiden Peak Shelter, built in 1999 by the Eugene Chapter of the Oregon Nordic Club. Inside (it isn't locked) you'll find a woodstove and sleeping space for a dozen or more people. It's quite comfy and will spare you having to haul a tent—if you get there in time for a spot!

ELEVATION PROFILE

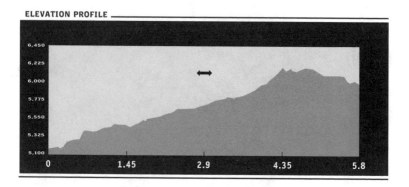

DIRECTIONS: From I-5 just south of Eugene, follow OR 58 for 62 miles east to the Willamette Pass Ski Area. Go another 0.2 miles east, then turn left, following a sign for PCT Trailhead. After 100 feet, turn right on a gravel road and follow it 0.1 mile to the end of the road. There's an outhouse here, and no fee is required.

GPS Trailhead Coordinates	10 ROSARY LAKES TO MAIDEN PEAK SHELTER
UTM zone (WGS84):	10T
Easting:	578410
Northing:	4827494
Latitude:	43°35.777'N
Longitude:	122°1.714'W

11 Wickiup Plain *to* Sisters Mirror Lake

SCENERY: ✿ ✿ ✿ ✿	DISTANCE: *15.1 miles*
TRAIL CONDITION: ✿ ✿ ✿	HIKING TIME: *9 hours*
CHILDREN: ✿ ✿ ✿ ✿	OUTSTANDING FEATURES: *Sparkling mountain*
DIFFICULTY: ✿ ✿	*lakes, moonscape plains, towering peaks, volcanic*
SOLITUDE: ✿ ✿	*craters*

This loop through the South Sister area is dramatic in several ways. It's volcanic, alpine, forested, moonlike, and watery at the same time. It can be a long day hike or a simple overnight, or serve as the basis of a multiday exploration of the Three Sisters Wilderness. All this, and the total elevation gain is barely 100 feet per mile!

🚶 Shortly after leaving the trailhead, enter the Three Sisters Wilderness and enjoy a little warm-up stretch of nearly flat forest. At 0.4 miles, stay straight ahead at a junction with the Elk-Devils Trail, which we will return on. Cross Sink Creek here, then round the southern edge of Kokostick Butte (*Kokostick* is the Chinook word for "woodpecker") and, at 1.3 miles, pass a pond to the right.

Just past 2.5 miles, traverse a clearing with a view left to Koosah Mountain (*Koosah* is a Chinook word for "sky"), and at 3.5 miles reach the PCT. Even if you're only day-hiking, you should turn left here to explore Sisters Mirror Lake—an odd name, since you can barely see part of one Sister from the lake. It's a lovely lake, though, and is one of several in the area. Look for a user trail to the right as you arrive at the lake; this one goes to the northwest shore of Sisters Mirror Lake, where you can find camping and another trail that leads to Lancelot Lake, Bounty Lake, and Denude Lake. All of these have camping, but you must be 100 feet from their shores and have no campfire.

If you're feeling energetic, or if you're camping in the area and want a nice view, consider putting in a few miles south on the PCT. It first passes Camelot Lake (apparently a Forest Service ranger thought

11 Wickiup Plain to Sisters Mirror Lake

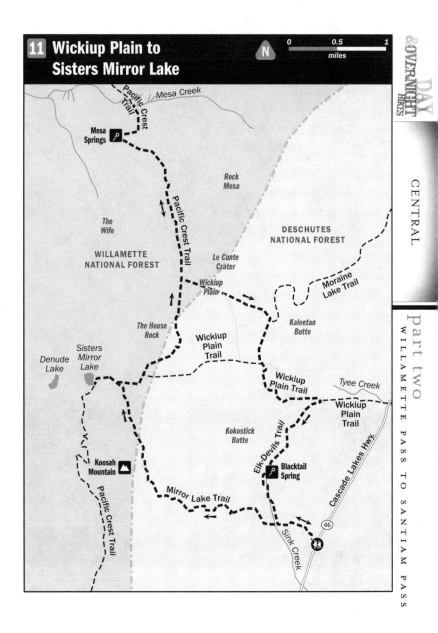

N

0   0.5   1
miles

Mesa Creek

Pacific Crest Trail

Mesa Springs

Rock Mesa

The Wife

WILLAMETTE NATIONAL FOREST

Pacific Crest Trail

Le Conte Crater

DESCHUTES NATIONAL FOREST

Wickiup Plain

Moraine Lake Trail

The House Rock

Wickiup Plain Trail

Kaleetan Butte

Denude Lake

Sisters Mirror Lake

Wickiup Plain Trail

Tyee Creek

Wickiup Plain Trail

Kokostick Butte

Koosah Mountain

Elk-Devils Trail

Blacktail Spring

Mirror Lake Trail

Cascade Lakes Hwy.

Pacific Crest Trail

Sink Creek

46

the area resembled a jousting field, hence Camelot and Lancelot),
then climbs 600 feet in 1.5 miles to the top of Koosah Mountain,
where a sweeping view takes in South Sister, Broken Top, and Mount
Bachelor.

From the junction of Mirror Lakes Trail, which you came in on,
the northbound PCT starts off to the east for a quarter mile to a
junction with Wickiup Plains Trail. You could go east here to cut
some distance off your hike (it's only 4.5 miles back to the car that
way), but the most impressive scenery here lies ahead on the PCT.
The trail now turns northeast, rounds the eastern side of The House
Rock, then heads north and into the heart of Wickiup Plain, a
pumice field thought to be about 20,000 years old.

With Le Conte Crater, Rock Mesa, and South Sister to your
right, The Wife to your left, and what looks like the surface of the
moon (but with flowers) at your feet, Wickiup Plain is a dramatic
stretch indeed. After 1.6 miles on the PCT, come to a stark intersection with a trail signed for Devils Lake. We will take that one back,
but I still recommend a bit more walking on the PCT. That's because
it's just 1.5 miles (with a small climb along the way) to where the trail

ELEVATION PROFILE

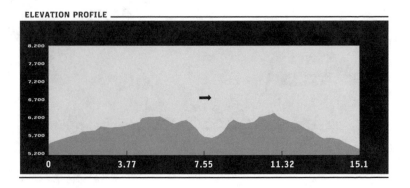

crosses a beautiful creek on the edge of a large meadow, and from here it's just another mile (and down 300 feet) to the two forks of Mesa Creek, the second of which flows through an exquisite meadow with camping to the left—a fine place to spend the night or just take an extended break.

Making your way back now, when you get to the junction in the middle of Wickiup Plain, turn left, following the sign for Devils Lake. Pass just south of Le Conte Crater (which you can scramble up for an interesting view) and, 1 mile later, turn right to follow a sign for Elk Lake. This is the Elk-Devils Trail, which you stick with for 3.1 miles (staying straight at 0.4 miles and turning right at 1.5 miles), all the way back to the original junction with Mirror Lakes Trail, at which point your car is 0.4 miles to your left.

DIRECTIONS: From Bend, go 30.1 miles west on Cascade Lakes Highway (FS 46) to the trailhead; a Northwest Forest Pass is required.

GPS Trailhead Coordinates	11 WICKIUP PLAIN TO SISTERS MIRROR LAKE
UTM zone (WGS84):	10T
Easting:	597631
Northing:	4874430
Latitude:	44°0.992'N
Longitude:	121°46.916'W

12 Obsidian Loop

SCENERY: ✿ ✿ ✿ ✿	DISTANCE: *15.9 miles*
TRAIL CONDITION: ✿ ✿ ✿	HIKING TIME: *9 hours*
CHILDREN: ✿	OUTSTANDING FEATURES: *Old-growth forest,*
DIFFICULTY: ✿ ✿ ✿ ✿	*lava flows, babbling brooks, flower-filled meadows,*
SOLITUDE: ✿ ✿	*soaring peaks, glaciers . . . basically, everything that's*
	good

This hike approaches the same destination as the Lava Camp Lake to Collier Glacier View hike, but from the opposite direction. Where that hike explores lava fields and lakes, this one winds through meadows and over babbling brooks. It's also the perfect introduction to the heart of the Three Sisters Wilderness.

🚶 When I close my eyes and think of beautiful places on the Oregon PCT, my mind wanders to the Obsidian Area. With alpine meadows, mountain views, crystalline waters, and soothing flowers, this is everything that hiking should be. And that's why it's gotten so crowded that you need a permit to go there. Call the McKenzie Ranger District, (541) 822-3381, or Sisters Ranger District, (541) 549-7700, for more information; permits are free.

Like so many good things in life, this section of the PCT also takes some work to attain. In this case, it's 5.4 miles from the trailhead to even reach the PCT, but those miles gain only 1,600 feet, and it's more than worth it.

From the trailhead, go 0.1 mile and turn right onto Obsidian Trail (#3528). Pass a turnoff for Spring Lake at 0.9 miles, then the grade gets a bit mellower as you climb into cooler forest. At 1.75 miles, come into view of a lava flow on the right, climb near it for a mile, then go onto it at 3 miles. Snake through the stone for almost half a mile and emerge at a crossing of White Branch Creek and a junction with Glacier Way Trail (#4336). This is the way you'll come back on the loop, so for now turn right, following signs for Linton Meadows.

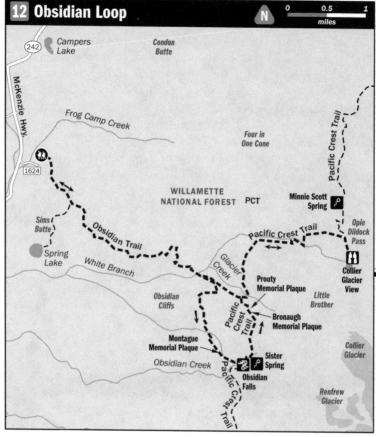

12 Obsidian Loop

N   0   0.5   1
miles

DAY &OVERNIGHT HIKES

CENTRAL

part two
WILLAMETTE PASS TO SANTIAM PASS

Over the next 2 miles, the forest opens up to reveal more and more meadows and views, and by the time you reach the PCT at 5.4 miles, you're at 6,400 feet elevation in a magical land of flowers and streams. You're also at a kind of decision point. I'm going to suggest a left-hand turn, but the area to the right is not exactly devoid of pleasures. In fact, my favorite spot in the wilderness, Linton Meadows, is about 3 miles to the south; it just happens to not be on the PCT. Still, consider camping on this hike and exploring all around.

For now, turn left (north) onto the PCT, and in a minute or two pass lovely, 50-foot Obsidian Falls. And about that obsidian: it may look like black glass, and in fact it is. It's a particular kind of lava that, if conditions are right, cools into this shiny material. It is profoundly illegal to take any of it home with you.

Beyond Obsidian Falls, and under a large cliff on the right, pass by Sister Spring and a series of small lakes. After topping a small ridge, look for a faint trail departing to the right and crossing a spring-fed creek; there's camping down there, and that trail goes up onto the snowfields of Middle Sister. So look for a campsite in the area (it must be at least 100 feet from trails and water) and go up that trail into the high country. Middle Sister is a nontechnical climb, but North Sister is a crumbly, technical, dangerous mess.

After a mile on the PCT, drop down to the upper crossing with the Glacier Way Trail, and a moment later a bridge over Glacier Creek.

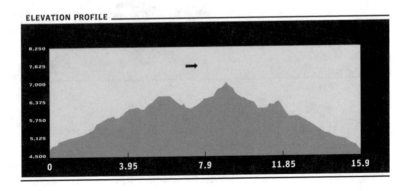

ELEVATION PROFILE

This area (6.5 miles into your hike) is known as Sunshine and is the heart of the area's alpine beauty. It's also generally closed to camping. If you want to cut a few miles off your loop, head back down the Glacier Way Trail here; otherwise, continue north on the PCT, cross the creek, and pass over a small ridge coming off of a peak called Little Brother. (The Three Sisters Wilderness also includes a Husband and Wife.)

One mile past Sunshine, the PCT reaches White Branch Creek and turns east to climb along it, and half a mile up it crosses the creek at a place called Sawyer Bar; there's camping on the north side of the creek here. Now it's back onto the lava for 0.6 miles to Opie Dildock Pass, from where another climber's trail goes 0.4 miles out to Collier Glacier View—truly a seat at the foot of the mountains.

To complete the loop, trace your steps back to Sunshine and head down the Glacier Way Trail. In 0.7 steep, downhill miles, reach the junction where the loop started, and from there follow Obsidian Trail 3.4 miles back to the car. You could also do a one-way car-shuttle hike and come out at the Lava Camp Trailhead by following the PCT 7 miles north from Dildock Pass, following the Lava Camp Lake–Collier Glacier hike backward.

DIRECTIONS: From Eugene, take OR 126 east for 56 miles to OR 242. Drive 16.7 miles up OR 242 to the Obsidian Trailhead.

GPS Trailhead Coordinates	12 OBSIDIAN LOOP
UTM zone (WGS84):	10T
Easting:	590266
Northing:	4895225
Latitude:	44°12.280'N
Longitude:	121°52.214'W

13 Lava Camp Lake *to Collier Glacier View*

SCENERY: ✿ ✿ ✿ ✿	DISTANCE: *14.8 miles*
TRAIL CONDITION: ✿ ✿ ✿ ✿	HIKING TIME: *10 hours*
CHILDREN: ✿ ✿	OUTSTANDING FEATURES: *Lava flows, alpine*
DIFFICULTY: ✿ ✿ ✿	*meadows, long-distance vistas, and a seat at the foot*
SOLITUDE: ✿ ✿ ✿	*of a glacier-draped volcano*

Take a tour through about as much variety as a trail can offer: thick forest, lava flows, craters, sublime meadows, and a glacier. With numerous camping options spread along the trail, this can be a challenging day hike or a great, exploratory overnighter. In fact, the south end of this hike is quite close to the north end of the Obsidian Area hike, so you could combine the two for a big Three Sisters adventure.

🚶🚶 One thing I can tell you, as a bit of friendly advice: don't do this hike in July. I'm assuming you don't like mosquitoes, or heat, or potentially losing the trail in the snow. Wait until mid-August or so, when the flowers are peaking and you won't have to deploy all your bug-avoidance maneuvers like the Charleston rest stop, the Jitterbug drink-of-water, and the hambone application of bug goop.

With that silliness aside, start behind the trail sign in the parking lot directing you to the PCT. When you get to the PCT, turn left and begin climbing very gently on a wide path covered with needles and cones, through thick forest and past the occasional meadow. Just under 1 mile, reach a junction for North and South Matthieu lakes. This is the old Oregon Skyline Trail and is also an alternate path taken by many PCT hikers, since the next 2 miles of PCT have neither water nor camping. You can take this route to add North Matthieu Lake to your hike, but even if you stay on the PCT, you'll be at its southern sister in less than an hour. There are campsites at both lakes.

Still on the PCT, you'll find at 2.1 miles that the forest opens up a bit, allowing views ahead and to the right of a ridge and lava flow.

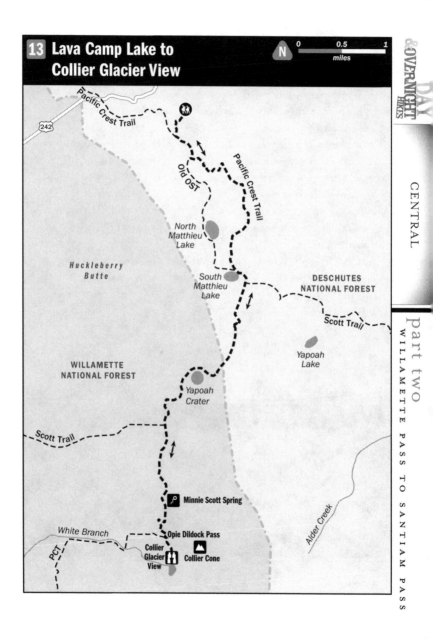

Pacific Crest Trail

242

Old OST

Pacific Crest Trail

North
Matthieu
Lake

*Huckleberry
Butte*

South
Matthieu
Lake

DESCHUTES
NATIONAL FOREST

Scott Trail

Yapoah
Lake

WILLAMETTE
NATIONAL FOREST

Yapoah
Crater

Scott Trail

Minnie Scott Spring

White Branch

Opie Dildock Pass

PCT

Collier
Glacier
View

Collier Cone

Alder Creek

The little saddle between the two is where we're headed now. In the next few minutes, look for views on the right to Mount Washington and Three-Fingered Jack, the next two peaks north on the PCT. The little bump out in the lava flow is Little Belknap Crater, which is another hike in this book. Keep looking, and eventually Mount Hood comes into view.

As you round a corner at 2.5 miles, catch your first view up to North Sister, the most crumbly of the three peaks. You can also see North Matthieu Lake below you on the right.

Three miles out, arrive at South Matthieu Lake, where the alternate trail from below rejoins the PCT. At the far end of the lake, Scott Trail (#95) comes in from the left and runs with the PCT for the next 2.5 miles.

Half a mile past the lake, get your first up-close encounter with lava, as the trail parallels a 400-year-old flow in an area that often has snow throughout July (we're above 6,000 feet elevation now). You'll get to walk on the lava for a bit (trust me, it gets hot in July) and find yourself walking toward the source of all this rock: Yapoah Crater, a reddish cone ahead and on the left.

ELEVATION PROFILE

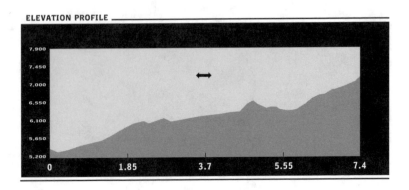

By the time you've put in 5 miles (and are at 6,500 feet), you'll have climbed around the southwest side of the cone and started down into lovely, greener country. The Scott Trail leaves to the west, at 5.5 miles, and just 0.1 mile later you enter a broad meadow with a creek and a million flowers.

Now we'll start our climb for the day—there had to be a climb, right? Look for Mount Adams, in the distance on your right, and flat-topped (and much smaller) Coffin Mountain on the left, which is way over by Detroit Lake. One mile past Scott Trail's departure (and 400 feet above it), come to Minnie Scott Spring, named for the niece of Felix Scott, the trail's namesake. There's camping for one or two tents on some flat ground west of the spring; no permits necessary.

Keep climbing, and within another 0.6 miles (and 200 feet) ascend to Opie Dildock Pass—and if there's any name in the book that needs explaining, it's Opie Dildock. The story goes like this: In 1932, a couple of Forest Service guys were looking for a way down into the White Branch canyon (just a mile south of here—the PCT crosses White Branch). When they finally found the right spot, they named it for Opie Dildock, an early-20th-century comic book character who always found a way out of tough situations. So there you have it.

From the pass, the PCT continues west, onto the lava, and eventually to the sublime Obsidian special permit area (see page 74). For now, we've done enough work, so enjoy the view of Collier Cone. Next, take the mountaineers' trail south from the 6,800-foot pass; you'll climb to the southern edge of the cone (about 300 feet up in 0.3 miles) and witness a spectacular view to Collier Glacier on the west side of North Sister. Also prominent here, really for the first time in your hike, is the north side of Middle Sister.

It's not too much more work (without your heavy pack, anyway) to further explore this area, aiming for either the saddle between Middle and North Sisters or the summit of Middle Sister itself. Climber trails abound, generally marked with rock cairns. Even if you pass on the climbing, you can't do much better than hanging out in this area for a little while.

DIRECTIONS: From Sisters, drive 14 miles west on OR 242 to the turnoff for Lava Camp Lake. Turn left, and in 0.3 miles stay right for the trailhead, rather than left for the campground. A Northwest Forest Pass is required, and there are no facilities at the trailhead.

GPS Trailhead Coordinates	13 LAVA CAMP LAKE TO COLLIER GLACIER VIEW
UTM zone (WGS84):	10T
Easting:	596964
Northing:	4901299
Latitude:	44°15.508'N
Longitude:	121°47.118'W

14 Little Belknap Crater

SCENERY: 🐾 🐾 🐾	DISTANCE: 4.8 miles
TRAIL CONDITION: 🐾 🐾	HIKING TIME: 2.5 hours
CHILDREN: 🐾 🐾 🐾 🐾	OUTSTANDING FEATURES: Lava flows and
DIFFICULTY: 🐾 🐾	mountain views
SOLITUDE: 🐾 🐾 🐾	

This little leg stretcher is absolutely not like any other hike on the Oregon PCT—or any other section of it, for that matter. For all but a few minutes, the trail here is on lava, and in fact you'll follow the trail up the flow to its origin, a small crater with a big view. It's a good one for kids, but not for lightweight shoes or folks with knee problems.

🚶🚶 All the lava around McKenzie Pass is relatively new—geologically speaking. The oldest you'll walk on here is 3,000 years old at most. As you'll see, very few plants have managed to colonize it, so save this one for a cloudy day or the autumn, when temperatures won't be so brutal. PCT thru-hikers tend to come through here in August and have been known to hike this hot, dry section at night.

From the trailhead, start out in a thin pine forest and follow the trail north toward a clump of trees about 0.3 miles ahead. This "island" of trees was missed by the latest lava flow, rather like an eddy in a river. The trail swings to the right of these trees, crosses the lava "current" for 100 yards, and then heads for a second island of trees. Note, as you wrap around the west side of this island, that the south side, which catches most of the summer sun, is quite a bit drier than the north side.

When you leave the trees behind for good, you've gone 0.8 miles, and if the immediate scenery is getting old, you can at least look back for nice views of Middle and North Sisters and Black Crater, as well as up ahead to reddish Belknap Crater, your destination's big brother.

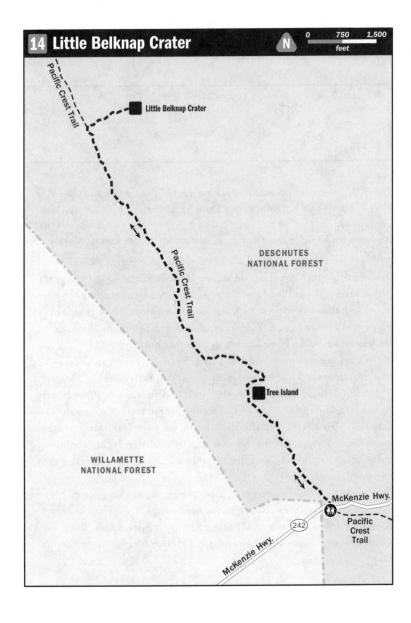

N

0   750   1,500
feet

Little Belknap Crater

Pacific Crest Trail

Pacific Crest Trail

DESCHUTES
NATIONAL FOREST

Tree Island

WILLAMETTE
NATIONAL FOREST

McKenzie Hwy.

242

Pacific
Crest
Trail

McKenzie Hwy.

The grade gets a little steep during this mile-and-a-half walk, but it never gets intense. Then, just before the high point on the trail, a rock cairn marks the side trail to the crater. Once you're on this ridge trail, you can look out to the north and see Mount Washington, which is what's left of a volcano after a series of glaciers got through with it.

The only really steep section of this hike is at the very end, where you might occasionally have to scramble a bit. In fact, this whole trail would be rough on a pair of regular shoes, so wear some stiff-soled boots.

From the top, your view extends from the rolling lava fields at your feet south to North and Middle Sisters, and of course Mount Washington to the north. Middle Sister is on the right, and the glacier on the left side of it is the Collier Glacier; the Lava Camp Lake–Collier Glacier View hike, which starts almost right across the highway, goes to a wonderful viewing point of that glacier.

Little Belknap might not strike you as a normal-looking volcano, but in fact it's what's known as a shield volcano—so called because it's said to resemble a warrior's shield. A shield volcano is formed by eruptions of highly liquid lava; since it flows so easily, it makes a long,

ELEVATION PROFILE

broad slope like the one you just hiked up, rather than piling up steeply. Three-Fingered Jack and Mount Thielsen are also (highly eroded) shield volcanoes.

DIRECTIONS: From Sisters, drive 15 miles west on OR 242 to McKenzie Pass. Half a mile west of the Dee Wright Observatory at the pass, turn right into the parking lot at a brown hiker sign.

GPS Trailhead Coordinates	14 LITTLE BELKNAP CRATER
UTM zone (WGS84):	10T
Easting:	595049
Northing:	4901447
Latitude:	44°15.604'N
Longitude:	121°48.555'W

15 Three-Fingered Jack

SCENERY: ✿ ✿ ✿	DISTANCE: *9.5 miles*
TRAIL CONDITION: ✿ ✿ ✿	HIKING TIME: *6 hours*
CHILDREN: ✿ ✿	OUTSTANDING FEATURES: *A ghostly postfire*
DIFFICULTY: ✿ ✿	*landscape, two mountain lakes, a soaring mountain*
SOLITUDE: ✿ ✿ ✿ ✿	*viewpoint, and a wonderful meadow*

Most day hikers never make it above Canyon Creek Meadows. And PCT hikers, hustling between Santiam Pass and the Mount Jefferson Wilderness, might not take much notice of poor, broken-down old Three-Fingered Jack. But it's actually a fascinating mountain, and this is your chance to get up close and personal with it—and also to see what a forest looks like after a fire, visit (and possibly camp at) two fine lakes, and stroll through a couple of wonderful meadows.

🚶🚶 If you get to the Jack Lake trailhead and see 25 cars, don't fret; very few of them are going where you're going. Most of them are doing a loop through Canyon Creek Meadows, which you will see. Others are camping at Wasco Lake, which you will also see. But very few of them are making the climb to the shoulder of Three-Fingered Jack, where you're going, for two simple reasons: they don't know about it, and there's a hill on the way.

Start by walking toward Jack Lake and following a trail around its right side. You'll be in a lovely, dry forest typical of those on the east side of the Cascades, and if it's sunny out, you'll feel it. Through the trees to the left, you can make out Three-Fingered Jack (allegedly named for a three-fingered trapper who lived in the area); our destination is just out of sight to the right of the summit.

You'll start climbing slowly through a forest that burned in the 2003 B&B Fire, which started as two fires, combined into one near this area, and swept through some 91,000 acres. But as you'll see

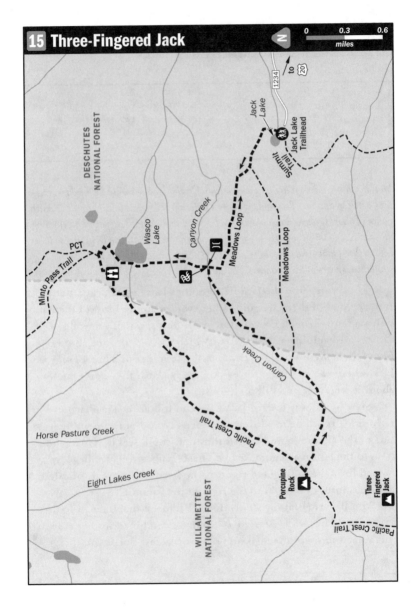

0   0.3   0.6
miles

DESCHUTES
NATIONAL FOREST

to 20
1234

Jack
Lake

Summit Trail

Jack Lake
Trailhead

Canyon Creek

Wasco
Lake

Meadows Loop

Meadows Loop

PCT

Minto Pass Trail

Canyon Creek

Horse Pasture Creek

Pacific Crest Trail

Eight Lakes Creek

WILLAMETTE
NATIONAL FOREST

Porcupine
Rock

Three-
Fingered
Jack

Pacific Crest Trail

during your walk, whole patches of forest were untouched, even though others were decimated. In some places, you can find patches of green in heavily scorched areas but also brown scorched spots in green areas. I spoke with a trail maintenance volunteer for this section, who said we can expect a lot more blown-down dead trees in coming winters.

Just under half a mile, you'll come to an intersection where begins the Canyon Creek Meadows Loop, a wildly popular walk with an interesting twist: the Forest Service wants the traffic to go in a clockwise loop from this point. So, technically, by turning right toward Wasco Lake, we're going the wrong way, but since we're not going to the meadows (yet), it doesn't matter (for now).

You'll keep walking through various degrees of fire damage and, half a mile past the junction, pass an impressive glacial erratic boulder on the left—so called because it was deposited here thousands of years ago by a glacier.

At 1.6 miles, you'll come to a second junction, this being the return of the meadows loop. Stay right, again for Wasco Lake, and a few moments later, you'll cross Canyon Creek on a rail-less log bridge between two waterfalls.

ELEVATION PROFILE

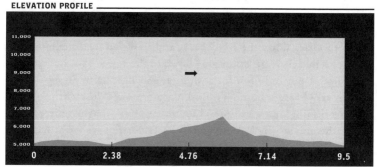

When you come to Wasco Lake half a mile later, you'll find a series of campsites along the left-hand shore, most of them in areas that were burned in 2003. The good (unburned) sites are at the far end of the lake, right where you'll turn left (and way up) on Trail 4015, which is labeled here as PCNST, or Pacific Crest National Scenic Trail—its official name. This trail picks up 200 feet in a fun quarter mile and deposits you onto the PCT at Minto Pass.

Follow the PCT to your left, which is southwest, toward Three-Fingered Jack, and in a few minutes you'll be rewarded with a panoramic view back toward Black Butte in the distance and Wasco Lake in the foreground—along with a whole bunch of fire damage. Again, note how the fire skipped whole patches of forest. Take a little break here, because the next few miles will pick up a thousand feet of elevation.

You'll climb for a little more than 2 miles to a minor saddle, where you cross over onto the east side of the ridge—a nice spot, but not the top. That's half a mile up, at the top of four switchbacks out on the open, rocky slope east of Porcupine Rock. From the top, at 6,500 feet, enjoy a grand view of upper Canyon Creek Meadows and the multicolored, many-layered north face of Three-Fingered Jack, whose summit is 1,300 messy, rocky feet above you. It is, in fact, the remnants of an ancient volcano. Another interesting feature is to your left: note how one side of Porcupine Rock burned and the other one didn't.

You could go back the way you came, but let's have a little adventure. Start back down the switchbacks and, just past the fourth one, look for a marginal trail plunging down to the right. Take it. It will be clear and easy to follow for a while, then will seem to disappear into an area of large boulders; find it again toward the right. Next comes a sloping, open hillside where you again stay right—but, at this point, the main thing is don't go too far left—and have faith. As the trail's steepness mellows out (the first half mile loses 700 feet!), just head for the sound of water, and when in doubt, aim at a notch on the left side of Three-Fingered Jack. There's a lake up there, and we will cross the creek flowing out of it. Also, look for a brown trail that comes out of woods at the far end of the meadow. Cross Canyon Creek where you can, then head for that trail.

This trail leads over a small rise, down through a lovely, narrow meadow, then down through a fine stand of mountain hemlock, and finally to the outer edge of the one-way meadows loop—a total drop of 1,000 feet in 1.5 miles. Here, you'll again see the one-way hiking trails. Going the "right" way, which is left, makes for a longer hike but will show you some beaver-worked trees on the trail to your left. You'll go 0.7 miles along Canyon Creek, which brings you back to your original trail, where you turn right and go 1.4 miles to the car; just follow the signs for the Jack Lake Trailhead, and you'll have a fine time.

On the drive out, if your feet are sore, stop and soak them in Jack Creek—or, I should say, see if you can soak your feet in Jack Creek. It is *cold!* And it is, therefore, just what you'll want.

DIRECTIONS: From Sisters, go 12.4 miles northwest on US 20 and turn north onto FS 12. Follow FS 12 for 4.5 miles, then go 1.7 miles north on FS 1230. Turn left (west) on FS 1234, which is pretty washboarded, and follow it 6.2 winding, bumpy miles to the trailhead at the end of the road. Northwest Forest Pass required.

GPS Trailhead Coordinates	15 THREE-FINGERED JACK
UTM zone (WGS84):	10T
Easting:	595872
Northing:	4927222
Latitude:	44°29.517'N
Longitude:	121°47.652'W

North

MOUNT JEFFERSON
TO
COLUMBIA RIVER

Pacific Crest Trail: North Region

N

0   9   18
miles

16 Pamelia Lake *to* Shale Lake Loop

SCENERY: ☆ ☆ ☆ ☆	DISTANCE: *16 miles*
TRAIL CONDITION: ☆ ☆ ☆	HIKING TIME: *10 hours*
CHILDREN: ☆ ☆	OUTSTANDING FEATURES: *[AQ]*
DIFFICULTY: ☆ ☆ ☆	
SOLITUDE: ☆ ☆	

This epic loop on the south side of Mount Jefferson takes in lakes, forest, sweeping views, alpine wonderlands, and some of the most scenic campsites you'll find anywhere. Note that if you want to camp at Pamelia Lake, you have to get a permit from the Detroit Ranger Station and use designated sites only. But the much better camping farther along doesn't require a permit.

🚶🚶 If you're looking for a two- or three-day loop to introduce you to a less-crowded corner of wilderness, try this one. You can also do variations on this, keeping it to as little as 4.5 miles (just to see Pamelia Lake) or using it as a starting point for exploring the southern Mount Jefferson Wilderness. If nothing else, the area around Shale Lake is worth exploring as a kind of less-crowded version of Jefferson Park, on the mountain's north side.

From the trailhead, start up a wide, barely climbing forest path along Pamelia Creek, named after a girl on an 1879 exploration party for her "unfailing cheerfulness." It would be hard not to be cheerful in a place like this. Around the 2-mile mark, look for a faint trail leading to the right to Flapper Spring, which is actually the outlet creek of Pamelia Lake, buried long ago by a rockslide. More on this later.

At 2.2 miles, reach a trail junction at the lake's southern edge. You can explore for a while, if you'd like, but by late summer, this lake isn't much to look at. Take the left (uphill) trail at this junction, staying on Trail 3439 toward the PCT. After another 0.8 miles of gradual climbing, reach the PCT on the edge of Milk Creek Canyon.

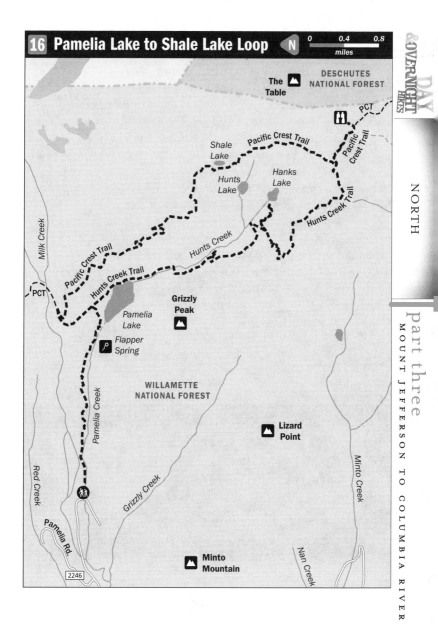

The Table

DESCHUTES NATIONAL FOREST

PCT

Shale Lake

Pacific Crest Trail

Pacific Crest Trail

Hunts Lake

Hanks Lake

Hunts Creek Trail

NORTH

Milk Creek

Pacific Crest Trail

Hunts Creek

PCT

Hunts Creek Trail

Pamelia Lake

Grizzly Peak

Flapper Spring

WILLAMETTE NATIONAL FOREST

Lizard Point

Pamelia Creek

Minto Creek

Red Creek

Grizzly Creek

Pamelia Rd.

2246

Nan Creek

Minto Mountain

This creek, named for its silt-filled glacial flow, is 0.2 miles north on the PCT; there's also a small campsite there.

Turn right (south) onto the PCT and round the west end of a ridge. Catching occasional views south toward Pamelia Lake, put in 3 unexciting miles before the grade lets up, the trail swings east, and another mile brings you to Shale Lake, in an alpine wonderland with Mount Jefferson looming just to the north. At 6.9 miles in, and with fantastic camping east and southeast of the lake, this is a fine place to spend at least one night. There are numerous other lakes to check out, and you might even find a climber's trail heading above timberline toward the southwest side of Jefferson.

South of Shale Lake, the PCT stays flat for 0.3 miles before dropping toward Hunts Cove, a dramatic bowl with two major lakes. The trail traverses the east side of the cove, passing under the Cathedral Rocks, and after 1.8 miles reaches a saddle and junction with Hunts Creek Trail (#3440). There's also a less-developed trail plunging into Hunts Cove, but it's steep and unnecessary, and by following #3440 you can get to the same place.

We'll head west here, but before that, it's worth making a 1.5-mile excursion south on the PCT to an amazing viewpoint that

ELEVATION PROFILE

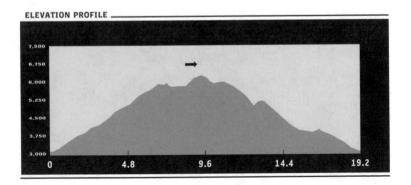

includes The Table and its volcanic surroundings—and, of course, Jefferson. There might not be a better view of Oregon's second-highest peak.

From back at the saddle, head west now on Hunts Creek Trail for a gradual descent of 1.6 miles to a junction with Trail 3493, which takes off to the south for Lake of the Woods and, eventually, Marion Lake. Now Trail 3440 plunges down a series of switchbacks to another junction, this one at the mouth of Hunts Cove. It's certainly worth exploring (or camping in) the cove; from here, Hanks Lake is 0.5 miles up this trail, and Hunts Lake is another 0.4 miles past that. There are fine campsites at both lakes, though Hunts gets less traffic.

Heading downhill from this junction, the Hunts Creek Trail now enters a flowery, water-filled valley that feeds into Pamelia Lake. There's just an amazing amount of water headed down these hills, which means it can get muggy in the summer, but there are also plenty of chances to cool off. Cross Hunts Creek 2 miles down (there's no bridge and you might have to wade), and soon you'll be at the upper end of Pamelia Lake. Working your way along the shoreline, you might notice that even with all that water flowing into the lake, there's no apparent outlet. That's because it was buried by that slide and now flows mostly underground. Hence, Flapper Spring.

It's 1.3 miles from the Hunts Creek crossing to the junction where this whole loop started, and from there an easy 2.2 miles back to the trailhead. And then, some 17 miles and 4,000 feet of gain later, you can go to Detroit and get a burger.

DIRECTIONS: From Detroit, head east on OR 22 for 12 miles and turn left (east) onto Pamelia Rd. (FS 2246). The trailhead is at the end of this road, 3.7 miles ahead.

GPS Trailhead Coordinates	16 PAMELIA LAKE TO SHALE LAKE LOOP
UTM zone (WGS84):	10T
Easting:	587929
Northing:	4945750
Latitude:	44°39.584'N
Longitude:	121°53.455'W

17 Jefferson Park

SCENERY: 🐾 🐾 🐾 🐾
TRAIL CONDITION: 🐾 🐾 🐾
CHILDREN: 🐾 🐾
DIFFICULTY: 🐾 🐾 🐾
SOLITUDE: 🐾

DISTANCE: *14.9 miles*
HIKING TIME: *9 hours*
OUTSTANDING FEATURES: *Old-growth forest, alpine meadows, rushing creeks, and a flower-filled wonderland at the base of Oregon's second-highest peak*

When one thinks of highlights along the Pacific Crest Trail in Oregon, the mind invariably wanders to Jefferson Park, with its lakes, meadows, flowers, and front-row view of Mount Jefferson. Two notes to consider, though: it gets crowded on weekends, and before August, you'll be in a fog of mosquitoes.

👫 Some day fairly soon, the Forest Service will probably have to limit access to Jefferson Park, as it does with the Obsidian Permit Area in the Three Sisters Wilderness. It's one of those ironies of the mountains: the places that are beautiful and easy to get to eventually get overused. What to do? Go during the week, especially after Labor Day, and don't go tramping around on the meadows. As you'll see, there are *plenty* of trails to use.

From the trailhead, start on a wonderfully gradual climb: about 1,500 feet in 2.6 miles. Though you can't see any mountains yet, the view is nonetheless sublime as you switchback up through a magnificent mid-elevation old-growth fir forest. After 1.5 miles of this mellow splendor, reach a trail intersection and turn right to stay on Jefferson Park Trail, #3429.

Keep climbing for another mile, passing a clearing with a view back down the valley of Whitewater Creek and rounding the southern end of a ridge. One mile from the junction, pass through a saddle and head for the southern edge of the Sentinel Hills, which you traverse with an ever-improving view of Mount Jefferson ahead.

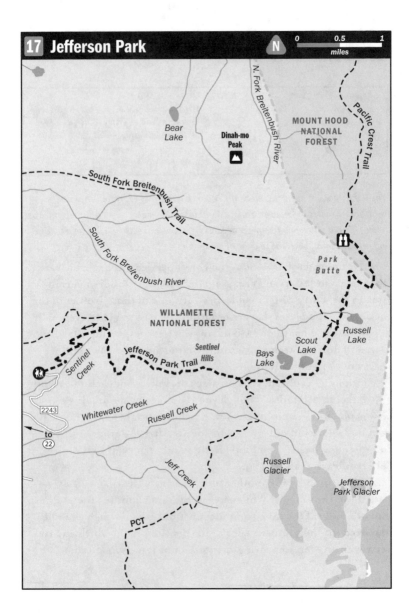

N

0   0.5   1
miles

Bear
Lake

Dinah-mo
Peak

N. Fork Breitenbush River

MOUNT HOOD
NATIONAL
FOREST

Pacific Crest Trail

South Fork Breitenbush Trail

South Fork Breitenbush River

Park
Butte

WILLAMETTE
NATIONAL
FOREST

Sentinel
Hills

Bays
Lake

Scout
Lake

Russell
Lake

Sentinel Creek

Jefferson Park Trail

2243

Whitewater Creek

Russell Creek

to
22

Jeff Creek

Russell
Glacier

Jefferson
Park Glacier

PCT

After 1.3 flat miles, cross Whitewater Creek and climb slightly for a quarter mile to the PCT, which from the south has just finished a 9-mile traverse of Jefferson's west side from Shale Lake—so, as you can see, it's possible (and recommended) to connect this hike with the Pamelia Lake–Shale Lake hike and/or the Breitenbush Lake to Park Butte hike. The walk from Pamelia Lake to Breitenbush Lake on the PCT is about 20 miles.

For now, though, turn left onto the PCT and follow its north-bound route gently uphill for a mile—and start getting used to all these flowers and meadows. In August, when the flowers are in full bloom, it's tough to tell it from heaven. Climb a final hill, swing around to the north, and it's Welcome to Jefferson Park.

The first thing you'll notice is there are a *lot* of trails. Few of them are official, however. The unfortunate reality is that so many people come up here that there aren't enough designated campsites for everyone (hence the plans for permits), so for now people just wander all over the place, looking for places to camp. Signs at the trailhead (and the staff at the Detroit Ranger Station) will tell you where camping is legitimate, but the general rule of thumb is if you're within 250 feet of a lake and *don't* see a campsite sign with a

ELEVATION PROFILE

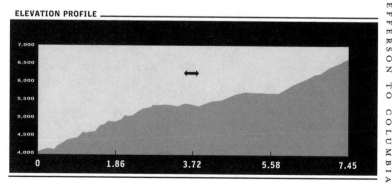

triangle, don't camp there. Fires are prohibited throughout Jefferson Park.

Still, plan on spending a night. Scout Lake, the first big one on the left, is quite popular. My personal favorite sites are on the far side of Bays Lake, west of Scout. Russell Lake, at the far end, is off-limits for camping.

Once you've found a site, or rested from the climb up, you have three general options: explore the lake areas, look for a climber's trail up onto the mountain that starts east of where you enter the basin, or follow the PCT across it and up to the top of Park Butte. (The mileage for this hike is figured as a round-trip to the butte.)

Along the way, you'll cross the South Fork Breitenbush River and its adjacent trail (#3375), and if you're looking for a nice way out of the wilderness, take this trail; it leads about 8.5 miles down to another trail that leads 2.5 more miles to Breitenbush Hot Springs. If you're looking for a good campsite, check about 50 yards past the (tiny) river.

Beyond this junction, the PCT starts to climb out of Jefferson Park, a 2-mile, 1,110-foot ascent that will put you on a spectacular vista point of Jefferson Park, Mount Jefferson, Mount Hood, and much of its namesake national forest to the north. This spot is also the southernmost point of our Breitenbush Lake–Park Butte hike.

If you're wondering about some of the names, Mount Jefferson is one of the few things around with a name bestowed by Lewis and Clark's Corps of Discovery; they saw it on March 30, 1806, from a spot near Portland's location and named it for the president who sent them west. Breitenbush (actually Breitenbusher) was the name of an early pioneer.

DIRECTIONS: From Detroit, go east on OR 22 for 10 miles and turn north onto Whitewater Rd., which is also marked as FS 2243. The trailhead is 7.4 miles ahead, at the end of the road.

GPS Trailhead Coordinates	17 JEFFERSON PARK
UTM zone (WGS84):	10T
Easting:	589098
Northing:	4950990
Latitude:	44°42.405'N
Longitude:	121°52.515'W

SCENERY: ⚑ ⚑ ⚑ ⚑	DISTANCE: *7 miles*
TRAIL CONDITION: ⚑ ⚑ ⚑	HIKING TIME: *4 hours*
CHILDREN: ⚑	OUTSTANDING FEATURES: *Meadows, rock*
DIFFICULTY: ⚑ ⚑ ⚑	*fields, late-summer snow, and a monster mountain*
SOLITUDE: ⚑ ⚑	*viewpoint*

This classic walk can be a moderately challenging day hike, an easy overnight hike, or part of a two- or three-day exploration of the area north of Mount Jefferson. If nothing else, extend it down into Jefferson Park and consider combining it with the Jefferson Park hike [x-ref]. You can't find a dull hike in this part of the world!

🥾 Hikers are funny folks sometimes. Everybody knows about Jefferson Park, and just about everybody comes at it from a trailhead down near Santiam Pass—and, faithful guide that I am, I describe that hike on pages [x-ref]. The Jefferson Park hike is easier, 'tis true. But this hike, to a ridge that looms 1,200 feet above Jefferson Park, is shorter, more scenic, *and* less traveled. Funny—and fortunate for us.

But before we start walking, let's give credit to the hardworking folks who maintain this section of trail: the West Cascade Chapter of Backcountry Horsemen of Oregon. The trail north of here is handled by, believe it or not, a group called the Oregon Mule Skinners. All this is on behalf of the Mount Hood chapter of the Pacific Crest Trail Association.

Begin the hike by following a short spur trail southwest from the parking lot to the PCT, then turn left in a series of meadows filled with lupines, daisies, and clouds of migratory monarch butterflies— all this in August, which is not only the best time to do this hike. but also the first month when you won't have tons of snow and hordes of mosquitoes.

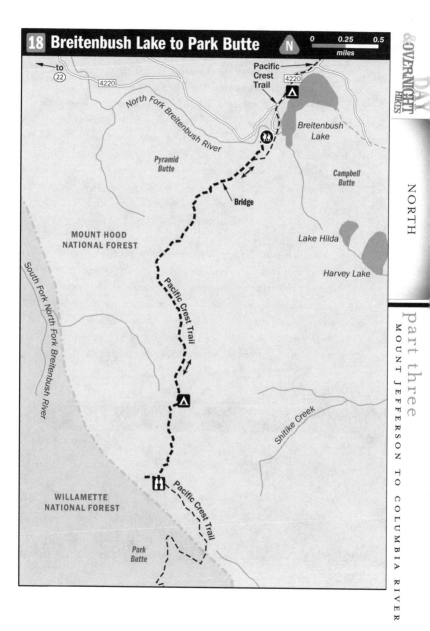

18 Breitenbush Lake to Park Butte

N

0   0.25   0.5
miles

DAY
&OVERNIGHT
HIKES

NORTH

part three
MOUNT JEFFERSON TO COLUMBIA RIVER

to 22

4220

North Fork Breitenbush River

Pacific Crest Trail

4220

Breitenbush Lake

Pyramid Butte

Bridge

Campbell Butte

MOUNT HOOD NATIONAL FOREST

Lake Hilda

Harvey Lake

South Fork North Fork Breitenbush River

Pacific Crest Trail

Shitike Creek

WILLAMETTE NATIONAL FOREST

Pacific Crest Trail

Park Butte

After 0.6 miles of easy strolling, take a bridge over a creek that typically runs dry by summer. However, from the looks of it (a deep, narrow gorge filled with large boulders), early-season hikers should get a real show of pounding water. On the far side of the bridge, there's a trail that drops down to the right; if you're into lung busting, this trail climbs Pyramid Butte, the pointy hill to the right of the trail. It's a 400-foot climb over half a mile, but much better views lie ahead on our trail.

At 0.7 miles, approach a rock slide with a sweeping view north, and at 1.5 miles, look for a fascinating and (to me, anyway) mysterious pile of rocks. I honestly don't know what this is, much less why someone did it. The elevation here is 6,100 feet, by the way—600 done and 1,000 to go.

Around 2 miles out, hike into an area that typically exhibits patches of snow well into July, even into August. The snowy ground inspires hikers to create multiple trails as alternates to the snowfields; just stay on the biggest one and watch for rock cairns or pieces of wood conspicuously sticking up out of rock piles. And remember, if you're going up, you're going the right way. The ridge you can make out just to the right of Mount Jefferson, up ahead, is our destination.

ELEVATION PROFILE

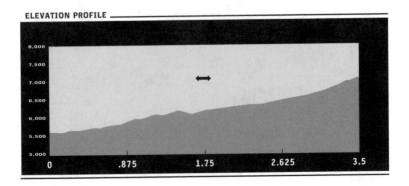

At 2.7 miles (and 6,400 feet), there's a small lake on the left and a campsite on the right with a metal fire ring. If you're looking for an easy overnight with the kids, this would make a lovely spot to pitch your tent. There's another lake 0.3 miles farther up the PCT with an inferior tent site on its south side.

The last half mile of this climb is in the wide, wide open: rocks, snow, sky, and big views. If there's a lot of snow and you can't find a trail, there should be plenty of footprints, and if not, aim for a notch on the ridge between two bumps; that's where the trail arrives up there.

And what an arrival! This hike saves its best for last. As you crest the ridge and look just a few miles south toward Mount Jefferson and the meadows, trees, and lakes of Jefferson Park curled up at its feet, you'll either go silent or say something like "holy mackerel" and then stand there gawking like a fool.

Jefferson, at 10,497 feet, is Oregon's second-highest peak and the toughest to climb. One of the popular routes is right up the Jefferson Park Glacier, which from Park Butte is just right of center. Farther right is the Russell Glacier, and the one draping the left side of the peak is the Whitewater Glacier. There's another glacier, the Waldo, around the other side.

Ever-popular Jefferson Park seems to sit right at your feet, but it's actually a little more than a 2-mile hike during which you lose 1,200 feet of altitude. If you're determined to spend the night there (and you should—just not on a summer weekend, unless you like crowds), think about coming at it from the other direction. See the Jefferson Park hike, an easy hike of about 9 miles round-trip; from this trailhead, it's closer to 12 miles with a lot more climbing.

Technically, the summit of Park Butte is about 200 yards west of you, a peak simply labeled "7018" on maps. Again, if you're one of those peak baggers, knock yourself out. I'm one of the folks who'd be sitting under a tree, eating cheese and crackers, enjoying the view just like it is.

DIRECTIONS: From Estacada, take OR 224 southeast for 25 miles to the ranger station at Ripplebrook. Turn south onto FS 46 and follow it for 30 miles to FS 4220, which is just before a set of power lines. Turn left onto FS 4220, stay right in a quarter mile, and follow (the now unpaved) FS 4220 for 6 more miles to the trailhead.

GPS Trailhead Coordinates	18 BREITENBUSH LAKE TO PARK RIDGE
UTM zone (WGS84):	10T
Easting:	596101
Northing:	495753
Latitude:	44°45.882'N
Longitude:	121°47.135'W

19 Olallie Lake *to* Upper Lake

SCENERY: ✬ ✬ ✬
TRAIL CONDITION: ✬ ✬ ✬
CHILDREN: ✬ ✬ ✬ ✬
DIFFICULTY: ✬ ✬
SOLITUDE: ✬ ✬ ✬

DISTANCE: *4.6 miles*
HIKING TIME: *2.5 hours*
OUTSTANDING FEATURES: *A series of mountain lakes with occasional views of big peaks*

This casual stroll through the lovely Olallie Scenic Area visits, or comes close to, about a dozen lakes. While it might not be dramatic or challenging enough by itself to merit the long drive, the area around Olallie Lake, at this trailhead, is the perfect place to spend a weekend hiking, camping, fishing, or just lazing around.

🥾 Most thru-hikers might not even remember this section of the PCT. On my thru-hike of Oregon in 2005, I ripped through here so fast I wouldn't have noticed a family of bears on the trail; that's because I had been on the trail for four days since Santiam Pass, and Olallie Lake Resort has ice cream and showers. It also has several campgrounds, cabins and boats for rent, a store, great trout fishing, and miles upon miles of trails. So what I'm saying is, go spend a weekend at Olallie Lake, and while you're there, check out this easy, lake-filled hike to Upper Lake.

From the trailhead, with your store-bought coffee in hand, follow the path up a short hill to the PCT junction on a ridge above Head Lake, which has a dock for swimmers to dive from. Take a left to head north on the Crest Trail and enjoy some nice, gradual climbing through a thin forest, with views of sprawling Olallie Lake to your left.

After half a mile, on a little bump of a hill, look behind you for a nice view of Olallie Butte, looming some 3,300 feet above the lake. A couple minutes later, arrive at a small campsite near Scharf Lake, and a minute past that, catch a view south to Mount Jefferson and a

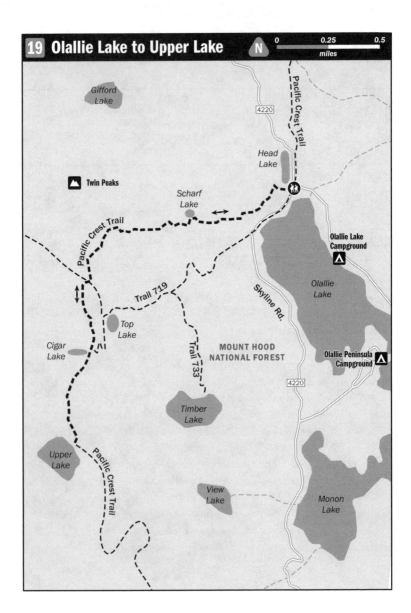

N

0   0.25   0.5
miles

Gifford
Lake

4220

Pacific Crest Trail

Head
Lake

▲ Twin Peaks

Scharf
Lake

↔

Pacific Crest Trail

Olallie Lake
Campground
▲

Olallie
Lake

Skyline Rd.

Trail 719

Top
Lake

Olallie Peninsula
Campground ▲

Cigar
Lake

Trail 733

MOUNT HOOD
NATIONAL FOREST

4220

Timber
Lake

Upper
Lake

Pacific Crest Trail

View
Lake

Monon
Lake

big burned area on the far side of Olallie Lake; this 2001 burn closed a big section of the PCT between here and Mount Jefferson.

Climb for another half mile or so (but only 200 feet), and at 1.1 miles cross to the right side of a small ridge, then into a thicker forest. You'll pass through a saddle on the south side of a rocky peak; it's the southern half of a pair with the clever name Twin Peaks. If you're into bushwhacking, there's a small lake between them, about a quarter mile northwest of the PCT.

When the PCT drops off the saddle, you will join Trail 719, a 3-mile detour north that takes in five more lakes. Downhill, it goes to Top Lake in a quarter mile, and from there trails loops back to the resort and also to Timber Lake. Did I mention there are a lot of lakes around here?

Staying straight ahead for Upper Lake, in just under half a mile you'll hit the southern end of the Top Lake Trail; stay to the right and uphill, and in a moment arrive at the long, thin Cigar Lake (another creative name). Beyond this lake, after a very brief climb, you've got 0.4 miles of meadow strolling to Upper Lake—passing on the east side of two peaks called, yes, Double Peaks. Why can't they be named Ernie and Bert or something?

ELEVATION PROFILE

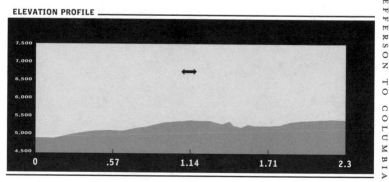

Just as you arrive at Upper Lake, there's a nice, big campsite on the right, and halfway down the lakeshore of the lake, a trail goes left a couple hundred feet to a meadow with more (but bumpy) camping. The best site, if you're looking for one, is at the far end of the lake, where a trail turns right and heads around the shore. A few hundred yards up, a trail goes up and to the left to a private site on a small knoll, away from the trail.

Note to the long-distance crowd: this hike lies just north of the Breitenbush Lake to Park Butte hike, which in turn connects to the Jefferson Park hike, which isn't terribly far from the Pamelia Lake–Shale Lake hike. So you could connect all four of those, starting at Olallie Lake and winding up at the Pamelia Lake trailhead, and it would be a total of just under 30 miles—a traverse of the Mount Jefferson Wilderness that would make a wonderful three- or four-day excursion.

DIRECTIONS: From Detroit, take FS 46 east for 25 miles to the intersection with FS 4690, where there's usually a large "Olallie" sign with an arrow painted on the road. If you're starting in the Portland area, this intersection is 45 miles from Estacada via OR 224 and FS 46, which you pick up at Ripplebrook. Either way, turn east onto narrow but paved FS 4690. The pavement ends after 6.3 miles, and 2 miles past that, turn right onto FS 4220, which leads 5 miles to the resort entrance. To reach the PCT trailhead, stay right at the Y junction and look for the parking lot 100 feet ahead on the right.

GPS Trailhead Coordinates	19 OLALLIE LAKE TO UPPER LAKE
UTM zone (WGS84):	10T
Easting:	595615
Northing:	4963018
Latitude:	44°48.850'N
Longitude:	121°47.445'W

20 Little Crater Lake *to* Timothy Lake

SCENERY: ☘ ☘	DISTANCE: *4.4 miles*
TRAIL CONDITION: ☘ ☘ ☘	HIKING TIME: *2.5 hours*
CHILDREN: ☘ ☘ ☘ ☘	OUTSTANDING FEATURES: *An amazing geo-*
DIFFICULTY: ☘	*logical oddity, old-growth forest, a pleasant stream,*
SOLITUDE: ☘ ☘ ☘	*and campsites on the shore of a large lake*

Hardly a wilderness area, Timothy Lake nonetheless does have some quiet stretches and backcountry camping. This hike visits some of those, and includes a trip to fascinating Little Crater Lake. And if you like having a forest to yourself, a nearby section of the PCT is your kind of trail.

🚶🚶 You start out in a big, beautiful meadow that seems as though it should be filled with deer and elk, though I've never seen either one there. As for Little Crater Lake, don't think you're heading for something that even remotely resembles the actual Crater Lake (which is in a caldera, not a crater). This is technically an artesian spring, which means that neither of Oregon's "crater" lakes is in a crater.

None of that matters, of course. Little Crater Lake is a jewel in a perfect setting, hidden away in a pocket of trees just 500 feet into this hike. It was formed when the earth cracked along a fault and water came up through a gravel layer to wash away soil on the surface. It's 45 feet deep, about the same distance across, and a constant 34°F.

Past the lake, follow a boardwalk over a stile and eventually through a cattle gate and into the forest. (The floor here will leave no doubt as to which side of the gate the cows live on.) It's just 0.3 miles from the trailhead to the PCT, which you join in a grove of big Douglas firs and rhododendrons. You could turn right here and enjoy a 3-mile walk in the woods, which you're sure to have all to yourself. Chances are, only a PCT thru-hiker or autumn mushroom hunter

113

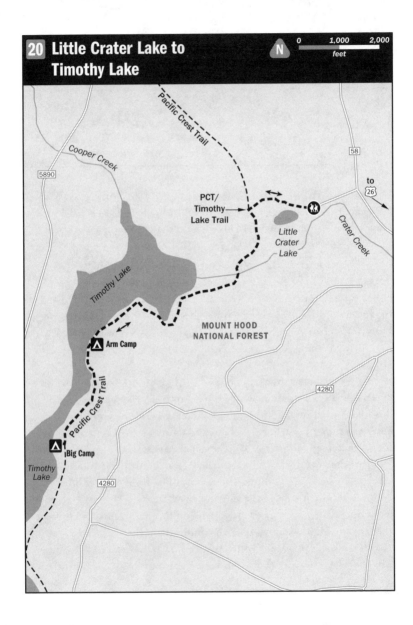

N

0   1,000   2,000
feet

Pacific Crest Trail

Cooper Creek

5890

58

to
26

PCT/
Timothy
Lake Trail

Little
Crater
Lake

Crater Creek

Timothy Lake

MOUNT HOOD
NATIONAL FOREST

Arm Camp

4280

Pacific Crest Trail

Big Camp

Timothy
Lake

4280

would be here, but according to one guidebook, the trees here include Douglas fir; western and mountain hemlocks; western red and Alaska cedars; silver, noble, grand, and sub-alpine firs; and western and white lodgepole pines. It's 3 miles to FS 58, and you could make a loop by walking back down the road 3.3 miles to the trailhead. It's 8 miles north on the PCT from our junction to US 26 near Frog Lake.

South on the PCT, in 0.3 miles you'll come to the Timothy Lake Trail, where you turn left and, in a couple minutes, cross lovely, swift-flowing Crater Creek on a big, wide bridge. From here, the PCT–Timothy Lake Trail heads through a virtual tunnel of newer trees, and 0.2 miles past Crater Creek you'll get your first glimpse of the Timothy Lake shoreline—or, in autumn, a stump-filled marsh where the lake used to be.

Soon the forest starts to open up a bit, the trees get older, and you'll be along a northeast arm of the lake. There's a campsite at 1.3 miles (0.7 miles past the creek) that's away from the lakeshore; better ones lie ahead. At 1.7 miles, in fact, there's a big campsite on the shore of a little bay, and a trail leads south along the shoreline to other sites.

ELEVATION PROFILE

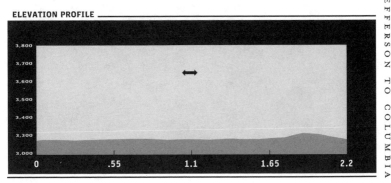

But the best lake access and camping are half a mile ahead, over a very small rise. When you top the hill and can see the main body of the lake through the trees, look for a faint trail leading down and to the right, toward a sprawling camping area. This place has good swimming, plenty of tent spaces, and a rocky point with a good view onto the main lake.

If you're wondering about the name Timothy Lake, it was named not for a person but for a grass. Before Portland General Electric built a dam and created the lake, a large meadow here was used for rangeland, and people sowed timothy grass to augment the food supply.

DIRECTIONS: From Government Camp, go east on US 26 for 12 miles and turn right (south) onto FS 42, following signs for Timothy Lake. Go 4.2 miles on FS 42 and turn right (west) onto Road 58, following a sign for Little Crater Lake. Turn into the Little Crater Lake Campground after 2.4 miles and follow the access road to the parking area at the far end of the campground.

GPS Trailhead Coordinates	20 LITTLE CRATER LAKE TO TIMOTHY LAKE
UTM zone {WGS84}:	10T
Easting:	598441
Northing:	5000133
Latitude:	45°8.870'N
Longitude:	121°44.866'W

21 Twin Lakes Loop

SCENERY: 🐾 🐾	DISTANCE: *4–8.5 miles*
TRAIL CONDITION: 🐾 🐾 🐾 🐾	HIKING TIME: *2–5 hours*
CHILDREN: 🐾 🐾 🐾 🐾	OUTSTANDING FEATURES: *Two mountain*
DIFFICULTY: 🐾	*lakes, old-growth forest, a nice view of Mount Hood*
SOLITUDE: 🐾 🐾	

There's not much of a challenge here, for either the day hiker or the overnight crowd. The total elevation gain averages less than 200 feet per mile, making this an easy-to-reach, easy-to-do introduction to the PCT in the Mount Hood area. And if you want to take the family backpacking without stressing them out, this is your hike.

🚶🚶 For the PCT crowd, Twin Lakes is a diversion used mainly for water or camping—and, even then, it's often ignored. Long-distance hikers passing through these parts are just a few miles from both a U.S. highway and Timberline Lodge, so there's not much here for them.

In fact, this trail was originally part of the Oregon Skyline Trail and, later, the PCT, but the PCT was moved up the hill when the lakes started getting camped out.

For you, what's here today are two lovely lakes and a nice viewpoint, all within easy reach. You can simply hike in to a lakeside campsite (a mere 4 round-trip miles of hiking), and in half a day you can see all the sights this area has to offer. And one other suggestion before we get started: consider combining this with the hike from Barlow Pass to Timberline Lodge, and you've got a one-way hike of just under 10 miles.

By the way, I did this hike once in mid-August and was in the middle of a monarch butterfly migration. This is something worth mentioning, because if you find yourself in the middle of this, it's

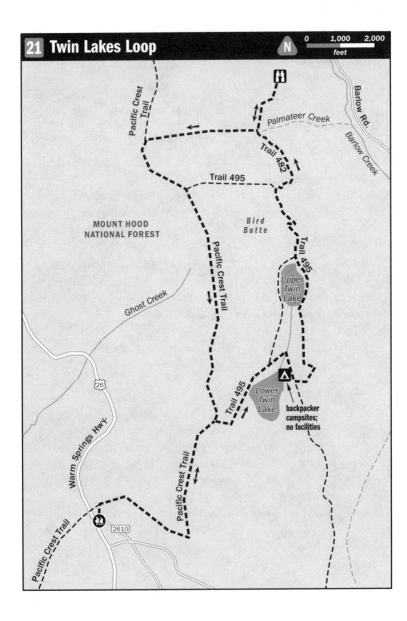

0   1,000   2,000
feet

N

Pacific Crest Trail

Palmateer Creek

Barlow Rd.

Barlow Creek

Trail 482

Trail 495

MOUNT HOOD
NATIONAL FOREST

*Bird
Butte*

Trail 495

Pacific Crest Trail

*Upper
Twin
Lake*

Ghost Creek

Trail 495

*Lower
Twin
Lake*

backpacker
campsites;
no facilities

Warm Springs Hwy.

26

Pacific Crest Trail

2610

Pacific Crest Trail

astonishing—hundreds of butterflies circling you. Also, the migration is fascinating, because the butterflies are born in California, fly to Oregon, lay eggs, and die; the ones born in Oregon then fly to Washington, lay eggs, and die; and *those* monarchs then fly to Canada, lay eggs, and die. Some of the ones born in Canada then return to California, often flying 100 miles in a day. Unreal.

From the parking lot at Frog Lake Sno-Park, head for the west end of the lot and walk into the woods near a hiker sign. You'll see a picnic table and garbage can here, and two outhouses are nearby. Go 100 feet and turn right onto the PCT, and take time to notice some evidence of the annual snowfall here: the height of the sign on your right, and the blue diamond marker on a nice hemlock on the trail. That's all related to winter sports; this trail is wildly popular with the ski-and-snowshoe crowd for its easy access and excellent grade.

You'll appreciate that grade as you head uphill on a highway of a trail, wide enough for two people to walk shoulder-to-shoulder, and of such a mellow steepness (gaining 500 feet in a mile and a half) that you'll hardly notice it—especially if the abundant huckleberries are ripe.

When you reach Trail 495, the beginning of the Twin Lakes Trail, turn right onto it, and soon you'll drop down a hill and see Lower

ELEVATION PROFILE

Twin Lake through the trees on your right. You'll also see a social trail or two plunging down the hillside to the shore, but don't use them; you'll add to erosion, and the main trail goes to the same place. After 2 miles (and a brief trip past the lake, up a drainage), you'll arrive at a junction with Frog Lake Buttes Trail at the northeast shore of the lake. There's camping enough for a village here, and also practically nothing alive on the ground, but there's also a trail that goes all the way around the lake, leading to other campsites along the way.

To head for Upper Twin and the rest of the hike, stay on Trail 495 and you'll round a bend, climb briefly, and in 0.7 miles come to a rocky area with a view, on the left, back down to Lower Twin, pleasantly set in its steep, forested bowl. Another quarter mile brings you to Upper Twin Lake and its own round-the-lake trail. Staying on the 495, you'll go along the east side of the lake, passing a big campsite from which a small trail goes into the woods on the right—to a toilet, believe it or not. Not an outhouse, mind you, just a toilet. Bizarre—and quite uncomfortable.

Upper Twin, by the way, gets less use, but that might be because it's smaller, much more shallow, and not well suited to swimming.

Half a mile north of "Camp Toilet," you'll come to a trail on the right marked "Palmateer View." Great name, huh? Sounds like a pirate or something, but alas, it's the name of a sheepherder from pioneer days. This trail is a shortcut to Trail 482, which you reach in a few minutes; turn left there, and you'll drop down to the headwaters of Palmateer Creek (probably dry), then climb briefly to a large meadow called Palmateer Camp. From there, a moderately steep trail on the right leads a third of a mile to the viewpoint.

This view gives you a unique perspective on Mount Hood, from the southeast, and the local stretch of the PCT. It climbs this side of the ridge on your left, drops off its end to Barlow Pass, then climbs to Timberline Lodge, the gray roof of which is visible from your viewpoint. That hike, and the next section north, are described here as the "Barlow Pass" and "Paradise Park" chapters.

You're also looking straight across (to the north) at Barlow Butte, with meadows on the side facing you. The drainage between you and the butte is that of Barlow Creek, traced by the historic Barlow Road, which was an overland portion of the Oregon Trail used by people who didn't want to risk their lives on the Columbia River. You can still drive this road all the way to The Dalles if your car has some clearance; it's accessed just off OR 35, at the trailhead to the Barlow Pass hike.

Descending from the view, turn right onto Trail 482 at Palmateer Camp, and in 0.7 miles it will put you back at the PCT. You're 1.2 miles south of Barlow Pass now, but to return to the car, turn left. You'll pass the upper end of Twin Lakes Trail 495 in 0.3 miles, climb slightly for just under a mile, then cruise the last 2 miles on the PCT, headed for the car. Pick some more huckleberries while you're at it.

Nice and easy, huh?

DIRECTIONS: From Government Camp, drive 7 miles east on US 26 to the Frog Lake Sno-Park. The trailhead is in the left-hand corner as you enter, and the sites left of it will be in the shade all day. Northwest Forest Pass required. There's car camping at Frog Lake, half a mile to the right from the parking lot.

GPS Trailhead Coordinates	**21 TWIN LAKES**
UTM zone (WGS84):	10T
Easting:	602081
Northing:	5009151
Latitude:	45°13.707'N
Longitude:	121°41.978'W

22 Barlow Pass *to* Timberline Lodge

SCENERY: ☆ ☆ ☆
TRAIL CONDITION: ☆ ☆ ☆
CHILDREN: ☆ ☆ ☆
DIFFICULTY: ☆ ☆
SOLITUDE: ☆ ☆ ☆ ☆

DISTANCE: *Up to 10 miles, or 5 miles with car shuttle*
HIKING TIME: *Up to 5 hours*
OUTSTANDING FEATURES: *Magnificent forest, solitude, a trip to the high country and Timberline Lodge*

It's hard to improve on a visit to Timberline Lodge, but here are two ways to do it: either walk east from the lodge on the PCT to some seldom-visited vistas, or climb up the trail through an amazing forest from OR 35, thus sweetening your arrival. The latter takes a second car or a 10-mile out-and-back walk, but it's the recommended route.

👫 There are more spectacular hikes in the Mount Hood area and on the Oregon PCT, but few have the combination of solitude, old-growth beauty, and mountain splendor this one has. It's also perfect for a picnic or just a dose of sunshine in a high-altitude meadow with Mount Hood looming over you. And if you do the one-way option with a shuttle, you'll end your hike at Timberline Lodge to enjoy its food, beverages, and historic setting.

From the trailhead, walk across FS 3531 and into the woods on the PCT. Stop to admire the relief map of the trail in the area, then take the left-most fork of the trails before you, walking north on the PCT toward Mount Hood. You'll take a few steps on historic Barlow Road, an overland alternative to the Columbia River back in the Oregon Trail days. After 0.1 mile along an abandoned section of the Mount Hood Highway, walk across the current (and quite busy) OR 35. The trail continues in a small draw on the far side.

The first part of the trail isn't too exciting; in fact, after 0.5 miles you'll walk through a fairly recent clear-cut. What follows, though, is a glorious stand of noble fir, with long, straight, branchless trunks. In June and July, wildflowers blanket the ground. In fall,

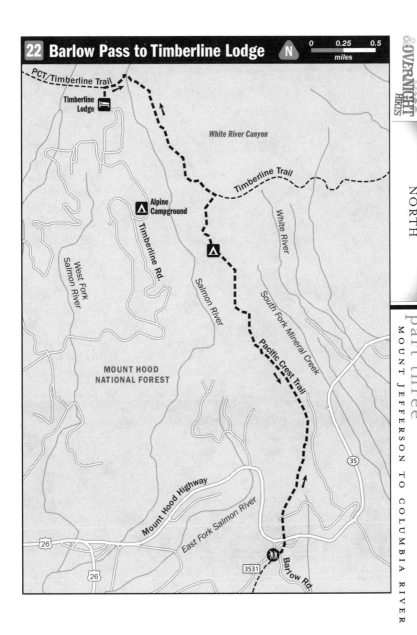

PCT/Timberline Trail

Timberline
Lodge

White River Canyon

Timberline Trail

Alpine
Campground

White River

Timberline Rd.

West Fork
Salmon River

Salmon River

South Fork Mineral Creek

MOUNT HOOD
NATIONAL FOREST

Pacific Crest Trail

35

Mount Hood Highway

East Fork Salmon River

26

26

3531   Barlow Rd.

DAY
& OVERNIGHT
HIKES

NORTH

part three
MOUNT JEFFERSON TO COLUMBIA RIVER

look for huckleberries and red-and-orange vine maple. Stay quiet, especially early in the day, and you'll hear birds and possibly see deer or elk. It's just a pleasant place to be, and the trail's altitude gain (less than 400 feet per mile) is entirely manageable.

If you're wondering about those blue diamonds on the trees early in the hike, they mark winter trails for cross-country skiers and showshoers. Their height should give you a sense of how much snow falls in these parts.

At the 2-mile mark, enter a more diverse forest, including a mix of firs and hemlocks. Cross a creek with a small campsite at 2.7 miles. Then, just over 3 miles out, reach an overlook of Salmon River Canyon and the headwaters of the Salmon River. The Salmon is the only river in the lower 48 states classified as a Wild and Scenic River from its headwaters to its mouth. The Salmon gathers its strength near the Timberline Ski Area and snakes down to the Sandy River along US 26. Facing west, note the rock patterns visible in a cliff face across the way; you're standing on layers of mudflow that burst from Mount Hood about 2,000 years ago.

Just after this point, the forest begins to open. In July and August, enjoy meadows filled with wildflowers, especially the spectacular bear

ELEVATION PROFILE

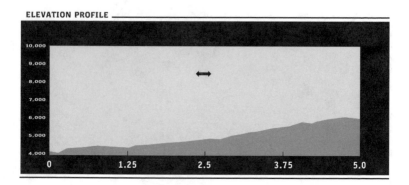

grass, which looks like a giant cotton swab. In a few minutes, reach the Timberline Trail (#600) in just such a meadow, with Mount Hood towering above you and purple lupines blooming all around. For the next 20 miles or so, the Timberline Trail (which goes around Mount Hood) and the PCT are one and the same.

Relax here if you'd like, and then turn around if your car is at OR 35 (for a total of 7 miles). You're at 5,300 feet elevation here (having climbed 1,100 feet since OR 35), and if you keep going, the next 1.25 miles gains you another 700 feet.

Otherwise, on you go, bearing left on the Timberline Trail/PCT, and in 0.3 miles find the first of several spectacular lookouts over the White River Canyon, which is 600 feet deep here. Look for buried 2,000-year-old trees in the mudflow along the far base of White River Canyon.

This section of trail is, in places, as sandy as a beach, and it tends to be windy above treeline, which can become tedious. If there's any rough weather in the vicinity, be prepared for the cold, regardless of the forecast. There's nothing to stop the wind this high on the mountain—wind that almost always blows in your face. I once hiked this section in snow and rain into a 30 mph wind with a full pack. Good times!

As you meander along the edge of the White River Canyon, you'll pass gnarled trees, cross meadows, and then ford the tiny Salmon River. This crossing has no bridge but is ankle-deep. Look for views south to Mount Jefferson, some 45 miles away, and a sign on the PCT with mileages to Canada and Mexico. You'll also encounter the Mountaineer Trail, which loops up to the Silcox Hut, then back down to the Timberline Trail west of the lodge (see page 127).

As you approach the lodge, trails shoot off in every direction, it seems, but the PCT eventually runs into a paved road that leads down to the lodge. Or you can just turn on your hot-chocolate radar and go for it; this is definitely a hike that finishes with style!

As I mentioned previously, it's possible to hike just the 1.5-mile upper part of this walk starting at Timberline Lodge—especially recommended if you have kids with you. This shorter option creates an easy, scenic alternative with very little elevation gain.

DIRECTIONS: From Government Camp, drive 3 miles east on US 26, then turn north on OR 35. Go 2.5 miles and turn right onto FS 3531, following signs for Barlow Pass and the Pacific Crest Trail. The trailhead is 0.2 miles ahead on FS 3531.

GPS Trailhead Coordinates	22 BARLOW PASS TO TIMBERLINE LODGE
UTM zone (WGS84):	10T
Easting:	603107
Northing:	5015159
Latitude:	45°16.942'N
Longitude:	121°41.119'W

23 Timberline Lodge *to* Paradise Park

SCENERY: ✿ ✿ ✿ ✿	DISTANCE: *5–13 miles*
TRAIL CONDITION: ✿ ✿ ✿ ✿	HIKING TIME: *2.5–7.5 hours*
CHILDREN: ✿ ✿	OUTSTANDING FEATURES: *Up-close views of*
DIFFICULTY: ✿ ✿ ✿ ✿	*Mount Hood, a dramatic canyon, wildflowers, and*
SOLITUDE: ✿ ✿	*waterfalls*

"Going through hell to get to heaven" might be a little extreme, but this is a pretty tough hike, especially since you have to cross a 600-foot-deep canyon twice. What's also true is that Paradise Park is about as nice as things get in Oregon. There are shorter options here, however, and if you make it an overnight, you'll find great camping.

🚶🚶 For the PCT thru-hiker, this stretch of trail is mainly about Timberline Lodge. Those words mean showers, laundry, resupply, a hot tub, and a legendary breakfast buffet. But for us day hikers and overnighters, Timberline is just a starting point. Our destination is a mountainside garden of flowers and water and stones, at the foot of a mighty volcano. Either a long day hike or an easy overnight, Paradise Park will reward your efforts with pleasant walking through fantastic scenery—after you've paid the price of admission.

From the parking lot, start out on the near side of the lodge, where a big sign says it's a quarter mile up to the PCT. And by the way, don't worry if you hear blaring hip-hop and see winter clothes in the parking lot; it's just summer ski camps, bound for the Palmer Glacier. Weave through the teenagers and head on up.

You'll follow a paved road up to a sign that says "Canada 550, Mexico 2108"; turn toward Canada and enjoy views of Trillium Lake, Mount Jefferson, the Three Sisters, and even faraway Diamond Peak—as you pass under two chairlifts and by a radio tower. There are various other trails and service roads that might confuse you; just stay on the wide, rock-lined one heading west, and you'll be fine.

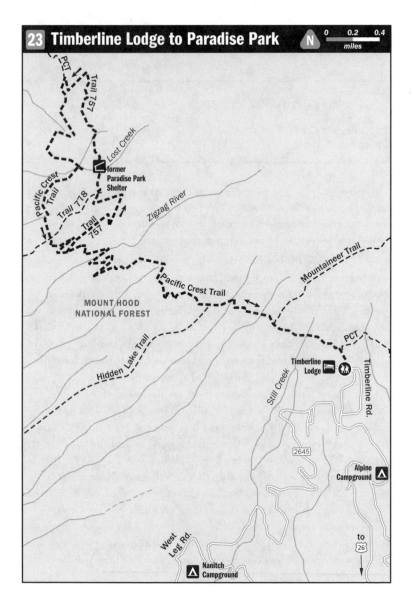

N

0   0.2   0.4
miles

PCT

Trail 757

Lost Creek

former
Paradise Park
Shelter

Pacific Crest
Trail

Trail 718

Trail
757

Zigzag River

Mountaineer Trail

Pacific Crest Trail

MOUNT HOOD
NATIONAL FOREST

PCT

Hidden Lake Trail

Timberline
Lodge

Still Creek

Timberline Rd.

2645

Alpine
Campground

West
Leg Rd.

to
26

Nanitch
Campground

After 0.8 miles, you'll come to the Mountaineer Trail, which heads up to historic Silcox Hut, and half a mile past that you'll come to a wilderness registration station. At this point, you've gone 1.3 miles and not lost any elevation; it won't last. By 1.6 miles, when you see the Hidden Lake Trail going down to your left, you'll be going ever so slightly downhill—something that often isn't noticed until one is headed home, some 11 miles later.

But who can worry about all that when you're winding through meadows and forests, past flowers and little springs? The best of these are around 2 miles out: great vertical bands of grass and color, the farthest one with a cool view of Ski Bowl and Tom, Dick and Harry Mountain.

Our first big Hood view since the lodge is at 2.4 miles, when you reach the top of Zigzag Canyon. If you have kids or have had enough, turn around now, because this canyon is something you have to go in and out of twice before the day is done, and in the bottom of it there's a river crossing with no bridge. See, straight across the canyon, in a brown patch on yonder hill, a trail winding upward? That's where we're headed.

Zigzag, by the way, is a name that comes from a pioneer's description of how he traveled through here: "turn directly to the

ELEVATION PROFILE

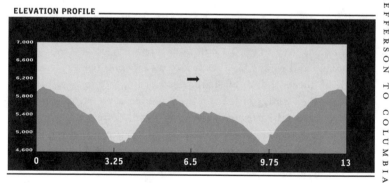

right, go zigzag for about one hundred yards, then turn short round, and go zigzag until you come under the place where you started from." You'll do something like that as you descend a series of switchbacks—let's call them zigzags—down 600 feet from the viewpoint to Zigzag River. I must offer praise to the volunteers who maintain this ever-sliding section of the trail, especially since they have to haul their tools around by hand. This section of trail also includes the only "weeping wooden wall" I can recall walking past.

When you get to the creek, you've gone 3.3 miles, and it's worth going up the creek a bit to see a waterfall farther up the canyon; I've also found the crossing up there to be better. Look around for sticks left by other hikers, or cairns at good crossings—two examples of good trail etiquette.

Funny thing about this hike: you climb out of this canyon on the sunny side in both the morning and afternoon! Something to think about as you start up. After 0.7 miles, take the Paradise Park Loop Trail to the right—that's if you want to climb up to the best attractions. If you'd like to take it a little easier, stay on the PCT for 2.1 miles to the lower end of our Paradise Park Loop, and you'll save yourself several hundred feet of climbing.

My recommendation, though, is to head up the loop trail (#757) toward, well, paradise. Starting around 5,100 feet at the junction, you'll hike up a side canyon to the northeast, through some intense patches of bear grass, cross a creek in half a mile, and then hike out into the clear. At a zigzag 0.1 mile later (elevation 5,200 feet), you can look up and see the high section of trail we pointed out from the far side of the canyon. A left-hand zigzag is at 5,500 feet—just keeping you posted—and, 1 mile from the junction, at elevation 5,700 feet, you'll cross the Paradise Park Trail (#778). Whew!

If you're camping, there's a social trail heading up toward the peak here, and folks camp up there—just keep it under the trees, and try to limit your walking in the meadows. Call this Upper Paradise. Staying on the 757 trail, in a quarter mile you'll cross Lost Creek, spy an amazing campsite on a ledge above it, and a hundred yards later come to the site of the old Paradise Park Shelter, one of several built back in the 1930s for people hiking the Timberline Trail. I find it ironic that a PCT guidebook raves that this shelter once had a working fireplace—and since that was written, the shelter burned down.

There are great campsites in this area as well, but the trail makes a right turn just before the shelter foundation and starts a long, wonderful, flat traverse through Paradise Park: heather, flowers, creeks, Mount Rainier, Mount Saint Helens, a big cliff above you called Mississippi Head, the Zigzag Glacier above that ... not bad at all for a flat walk. After 1.2 miles of this, you'll drop down into the forest again and intersect the PCT; this area has great views down the Sandy River Canyon, a literal cross-section of Mount Hood.

To the right, the PCT starts a 3-mile, 2,200-foot drop to its crossing of the Sandy, which can be quite the adventure; I can attest that doing that section in snow and rain with a sprained ankle is not fun. Just beyond that is Ramona Falls, which I mention only because an interesting feature of the PCT is that it gives you a new perspective on where things are in relation to each other; that is, most Oregon hikers know about Timberline Lodge and Ramona Falls, but only a PCT hiker would think about them being less than a day's walk from one another.

Turn left here, and we'll start back toward the lodge. After an easy half mile, you'll come to Rushing Water Creek and its wonderful canyon, where you pass just under its waterfall; below you is an amazing slot canyon and a view down into the Sandy River Canyon. Another half mile, starting slightly downhill now, brings you back to Lost Creek. Look for a trail that leads uphill just after the crossing; it leads first to a little double waterfall, then to a magical, hidden cove with yet another waterfall. They're everywhere! It's not hard to find campsites in this area either.

Another 0.7 miles brings you to the lower end of the Paradise Park Trail, where a horse corral will encourage you to keep moving. You'll really start downhill now, and in 0.4 miles come back to the junction where your loop started, the Paradise Park Loop Trail, #757. Follow the PCT back down into the canyon, and, well, hate to tell you, but from here—with 9.5 miles under your belt—you've 3.5 miles to go, gaining 1,200 feet, and you've seen it all before.

But, hey, it was worth it, right? Besides, you've got Timberline Lodge to enjoy now. The hot chocolate and coffee drinks are sublime, the food's not bad (or cheap), there's an interesting film about the lodge's construction, and its main lobby is about as nice a place to recover from a hike as you could ask for. And you deserve it.

DIRECTIONS: From Government Camp, go east on US 26 for 1 mile to Timberline Rd., which leads 6 miles up to the parking lot. From the lot, just walk toward the old lodge until you see the trail sign on the near side.

GPS Trailhead Coordinates	23 TIMBERLINE LODGE TO PARADISE PARK
UTM zone (WGS84):	10T
Easting:	601041
Northing:	5020512
Latitude:	45°19.850'N
Longitude:	121°42.633'W

SCENERY: 🏕 🏕 🏕 🏕
TRAIL CONDITION: 🏕 🏕
CHILDREN: 🏕 🏕 🏕
DIFFICULTY: 🏕 🏕 🏕
SOLITUDE: 🏕 🏕
DISTANCE: *13.7 miles*

HIKING TIME: *8 hours*
OUTSTANDING FEATURES: *A historic cabin, lovely waterfall, high-elevation forest, some route finding, a seat at the foot of Mount Hood, and a wonderful viewing point.*

The lower part of this hike, the trip to Ramona Falls, is well known to hikers in this area. But the real treats here are on a former (but still popular) section of the PCT that wraps around the headwaters of the Muddy Fork of the Sandy River, a destination that's much nicer than it sounds.

🏃 This hike starts on a trail that looks like a highway; that's because thousands of people make the trek to Ramona Falls every year. If you're looking for just a quick outing, or you have kids with you, consider that loop for a 7-mile excursion that won't leave you too winded.

One thing to consider, though, is that 1.2 miles up you'll have to cross the Sandy River, and the bridge there is only in place from mid-May to mid-October. There are often fallen trees to help you cross without the bridge, and it can be waded when low, but it's worth a call to the Forest Service to get the latest info.

Starting out from the trailhead, in 0.2 miles cross the Sandy River Trail, a connector from the Riley Horse Camp. Keep going on Trail 797 to Ramona Falls and admire a very large, cracked boulder near the junction. A short walk later, you'll see a nice view of Mount Hood upstream. It gets better.

After the Sandy River crossing mentioned above, walk a quarter mile to the PCT junction and turn right (south). Continue the gradual climb over moss-covered ground and under some very large

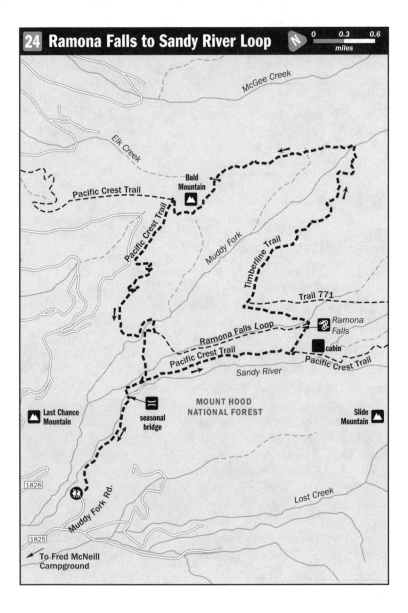

N

0	0.3	0.6
miles

McGee Creek

Elk Creek

Pacific Crest Trail

Bald
Mountain

Pacific Crest Trail

Muddy Fork

Timberline Trail

Trail 771

Ramona
Falls

Ramona Falls Loop

cabin

Pacific Crest Trail

Pacific Crest Trail

Sandy River

Last Chance
Mountain

seasonal
bridge

MOUNT HOOD
NATIONAL FOREST

Slide
Mountain

1828

Muddy Fork Rd.

1825

To Fred McNeill
Campground

Lost Creek

rhododendrons, and 1 mile up reach the top of a bluff from which the Sandy, below to the right, is more audible. Also keep an eye out for eroded cliffs across the way, offering a cross section of Mount Hood's volcanic deposits.

An easy 1.5 miles from where you joined it, the PCT dips to the right and toward the river; follow this for a little scenic turnoff. At the bottom of a brief descent, reach a campsite near the shore of the Sandy; the crossing here is known for being treacherous, especially for the early-season PCT crowd. But we don't have to deal with that. At the far end of the campsite, look for log steps leading up the hill to a 1935 ranger station, built to keep hikers on the Timberline Trail out of the protected Bull Run watershed. Rangers are no longer stationed here, but hikers can spend the night—though it looks like a haven for mice, and there's no guarantee the roof will keep the rain out. There are some tent sites nearby, though, as well as a nice view of the Sandy River Canyon about 100 yards uphill.

Follow the PCT back up the hill to the Ramona Falls Loop, turn right, and in 0.2 miles come to a horse gate protecting the entrance to the falls area. From here, you can drop down to the left to find campsites; no camping is allowed at the falls. Pass through the gate

ELEVATION PROFILE

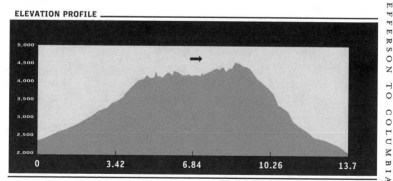

and enjoy yourself at the wonderful falls, which have always reminded me of one of those pyramids of champagne glasses. It's just amazing what such a small creek turns into when it falls off a cliff.

Continue over the bridge and at the far end reach a junction. To head back to the car, stay straight, but for our big loop, turn right and climb into a classic forest. You're rounding the end of Yocum Ridge on the Timberline Trail, which goes around Mount Hood for 42 miles. Technically, this is no longer the PCT—it was rerouted because this section couldn't be maintained for horses—but most PCT hikers take this slightly longer route for its scenery and more gradual climbs.

After climbing for 0.7 miles, reach the west end of the ridge and find Trail 771 heading east and up Yocum Ridge. If you're curious, this trail leads 4.7 miles to the 6,200-foot elevation in a dramatic alpine landscape at the base of the Sandy Glacier. You have to put in about 2 miles to get out of the forest. The name Yocum, by the way, honors an early-20th-century Mount Hood climbing guide.

From that junction, our trail becomes darn near flat, winding in and out of gullies and across small creeks. This north-facing section will have snow as late as July and as early as October. After an easy 2.5 miles of this ambling, you'll come to the first branch of the Muddy Fork, where a small clearing on the trail includes some nice camp-sites. If you're doing this hike as an overnight, these sites are your best bet for camping.

This is also where the trail gets more entertaining, in a kind of adventurous way. Your progress will be slowed as you have to pick your way through thick alder and over rocks. The trail is marked in places by rock cairns and/or ribbons, and the stream crossings aren't treacherous, so just keep trending level and enjoy the views of Hood and the Sandy Glacier looming over you. As you look up at the mountain, the forested ridge on your left is topped by McNeil Point, a popular destination on the Timberline Trail.

At the far end of this slide area, cross the main stem of the Muddy Fork (where your feet might get a little wet) and reenter the woods in an area where damage from slides is quite apparent. Now you have an easy, viewless traverse of 2 miles to the spectacular, flower-covered lookout on the side of Bald Mountain.

Just under a half mile past the viewing point, you'll come to a major intersection of trails. The first one, on the left, is what we want: the PCT heading south. From here, the PCT continues north to Lolo Pass, and the Timberline Trail goes back to the east and climbs toward the flowery heavens of McNeil Point, Cairn Basin, and Elk Cove.

Southbound on the PCT, things get a smidge tedious, as you drop 1,500 feet in 2.3 miles of switchbacks, with nothing to see until you arrive back at the Muddy Fork. Another bridge here was destroyed, so until it's fixed you follow a diversion up and down through a swampy, cedar-filled area to the new bridge, which at least offers a parting shot of Mount Hood.

Just 150 feet past that bridge, pop out at the Ramona Falls Loop, follow it right 0.1 mile to the PCT, then take a left there and retrace your steps 1.4 miles to the car.

A note for the long-distance crowd: this is the northernmost of four hikes in this book that trace the PCT's path past Mount Hood. You could make a fine, long hike by combining them all: start with the Twin Lakes Loop, trek north onto the Barlow Pass hike to Timberline Lodge, keep going onto the Paradise Park hike, then follow the long, pounding descent to the Sandy River. Make that (often sketchy) crossing, and you'll be at the site of the historic ranger cabin mentioned here. Then follow this loop around to the junction near Bald Mountain and keep going on the PCT to the paved road at Lolo Pass. From the Twin Lakes trailhead on US 26 to Lolo Pass, it's 26 miles one way on the PCT. It's tough to think of a finer two- to four-day trip.

DIRECTIONS: From Sandy, go east on US 26 for 17 miles to Zigzag, then turn left (north) onto Lolo Pass Rd., which is 0.6 miles past milepost 41. Go 4.2 miles and turn right onto FS 1825, which is 0.1 mile past a Mount Hood National Forest sign and marked "campgrounds and trailheads." Stay right at 0.7 miles, cross a bridge, and continue another 1.7 miles to turn left onto Spur Road 100, which leads 0.5 miles to the trailhead.

GPS Trailhead Coordinates	24 RAMONA FALLS TO SANDY RIVER LOOP
UTM zone (WGS84):	10T
Easting:	591448
Northing:	5026602
Latitude:	45°23.218'N
Longitude:	121°49.910'W

25 Lost Lake *to* Buck Peak

SCENERY: ✿ ✿ ✿
TRAIL CONDITION: ✿ ✿ ✿
CHILDREN: ✿ ✿ ✿ ✿
DIFFICULTY: ✿ ✿ ✿
SOLITUDE: ✿ ✿

DISTANCE: *16 miles*
HIKING TIME: *8 hours*
OUTSTANDING FEATURES: *A large lake, old-growth forest, solitude, and a mountain panorama*

Although the PCT doesn't actually visit Lost Lake, the lake and the easy trail around it (which you'll hike here) are well worth a visit. And the nearby stretch of the Crest Trail offers easy walking and remote camping in a beautiful forest, with a nice view at the end.

🚶🚶 Like the hike from Olallie Lake to Upper Lake, this one is as much about the trailhead area as the PCT itself. Lost Lake, with its stocked trout and famous postcard view of Mount Hood, has camping and cabins and boat rentals as well as an easy, 3.3-mile trail around its shore. Consider doing this hike as part of a weekend at the lake, or as a fairly easy overnight backpack. Either way, it's a glimpse into what many PCT hikers experience on a trek across Oregon: easy walking through beautiful forest, with almost nobody around.

Start in front of the store at the Lost Lake Resort and look for the Lost Lake Trail heading to your right along the shore. Pass by a series of picnic sites, and in a quarter mile you'll come to a viewing platform with a view of Hood across the way. If this particular view looks familiar, it's because you've probably seen it on a hundred calendars.

Continuing around the lake among big trees and countless huckleberries, look for a gigantic hollowed-out cedar just under a mile along; note that it's still alive at the top. Pass a boathouse a moment later with a tiny dock on the lake; at 1.6 miles a rockslide offers a fine swimming hole. At the 2-mile mark, the unsigned Huckleberry Mountain Trail heads up to the right; this is your path to the PCT—though there's nothing in the area called Huckleberry Mountain.

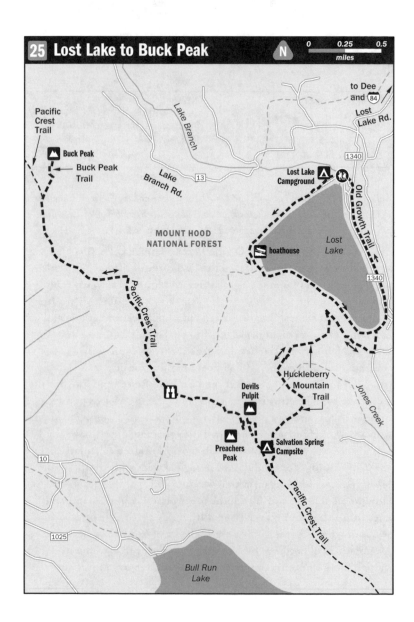

N

0   0.25   0.5
miles

Pacific
Crest
Trail

Buck Peak

Buck Peak
Trail

Lake Branch

to Dee
and 84

Lost
Lake Rd.

1340

Lost Lake
Campground

Lake
Branch Rd.

13

Old Growth Trail

MOUNT HOOD
NATIONAL FOREST

boathouse

Lost
Lake

1340

Pacific Crest Trail

Huckleberry
Mountain
Trail

Jones Creek

Devils
Pulpit

Preachers
Peak

Salvation Spring
Campsite

10

Pacific Crest Trail

1025

Bull Run
Lake

In just a few moments, you'll see a series of campsites along this trail, and a quarter mile up from the lake, the trail almost touches a road before switching back to the right and starting to climb among numerous rhododendrons. After a mile that picks up 700 feet (a rockslide on the right marks the top), catch a break with a mostly flat mile to the junction with the PCT.

Turn right, or north, on the PCT, and after a minute's walk come to a large campsite at Salvation Spring, which a handwritten sign calls "Salvatoin Spring." Now the trail climbs gently for a mile through towering forest to a saddle between Preachers Peak and Devils Pulpit. A Forest Service ranger named the former for his dad, a local preacher with a bum foot who rode a horse to the summit, and the latter got its name because somebody remarked that if a preacher is here, the devil can't be far away.

Passing between those peaks, the PCT offers views of Lost Lake and Mount Adams to the east as it loses elevation for half a mile to a rock pile on the left. Here, you can scramble up for a rare view west into Bull Run watershed, the uncut, off-limits drainage that supplies Portland with its water. From this rocky point, you can just make out Bull Run Lake off to the left.

ELEVATION PROFILE

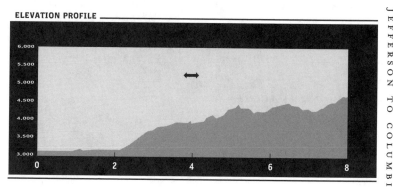

At a total of 6.8 miles since the trailhead (about 2.5 miles since you got on the PCT), you'll round a ridge where the view north takes in a large bowl with two peaks at the far end; the one on the right is our destination, Buck Peak. Work your way around the bowl, and 1 mile north from the viewing point, an unsigned, brushy trail heads up to the right; this is your half-mile-long summit trail.

The view from 4,751-foot Buck Peak takes in Mounts Hood, Adams, Jefferson, and Defiance (the forested one with the radio towers), as well as Lost Lake and the upper parts of the Hood River Valley. Along the summit to the left are the rusty remains of an old lookout tower in a small meadow that makes a fine picnic site.

On your way back via Lost Lake, turn right on the round-the-lake trail and enjoy the Old Growth Trail, a boardwalk with interpretive signs about ancient forests. You can also enjoy the view from Lost Lake Butte, a 2-mile stroll that climbs 1,200 feet to a nice view of Mount Hood. Then go back to the store and enjoy some ice cream.

DIRECTIONS: From Exit 62 (West Hood River) on I-84, turn right onto Country Club Rd., following signs for several wineries. At the end of this road, 3 miles later, turn left onto Barrett Dr. Follow Barrett for 1.2 miles and turn right onto Tucker Rd., the second stop sign you'll come to on Barrett Dr. Go 2 miles up Tucker and turn right onto Dee Hwy., where a sign actually says Parkdale. After 6.5 miles on Dee Hwy., turn right again, following signs for Lost Lake. Cross a bridge, take a left onto Lost Lake Rd., and follow it for 14 miles to the resort entrance.

GPS Trailhead Coordinates	25 LOST LAKE TO BUCK PEAK
UTM zone (WGS84):	10T
Easting:	592317
Northing:	5038742
Latitude:	45°29.780'N
Longitude:	121°49.129'W

26 Chinidere Mountain

SCENERY: ⭐ ⭐ ⭐ ⭐	DISTANCE: *4 miles*
TRAIL CONDITION: ⭐ ⭐ ⭐ ⭐	HIKING TIME: *2.5 hours*
CHILDREN: ⭐ ⭐ ⭐	OUTSTANDING FEATURES: *A lovely lake and a*
DIFFICULTY: ⭐ ⭐	*magnificent panoramic viewpoint*
SOLITUDE: ⭐ ⭐	

If you start in Portland, you might spend more time in the car than on the trail for this one. But the view from the top of Chinidere is more than worth it, and Wahtum Lake is a fine destination as well. Still, consider making this a part of a longer trip to Lost Lake or the Hood River Valley.

🚶 If you're measuring hikes with a view-for-effort scale, Chinidere Mountain would rank an 11 out of 10—once you get there. It's almost a 2-hour drive from Portland, but it's all paved, and you'll be rewarded with a fairly easy hike, a beautiful mountain lake with camping and fishing, and a view that stretches hundreds of miles.

If you're wondering, it's pronounced "SHI-na-dere," and it's named for the last reigning chief of the local Wasco tribe. And *Wahtum* is a word from a local native tongue meaning pond or body of water. So you're looking through the trees here at Lake Lake.

From the trailhead, proceed through the campground (not down the road near the outhouse) and follow a trail called the Wahtum Express—so called because it includes 250 steps. (You can skip this by following a parallel horse trail to the right, if you wish.) At the bottom of the Express, turn left and walk 100 feet down to a big tree with two PCT signs on it. You'll be right by the lake, with a picnic area in front of you—and also in the middle of several nice lakeshore campsites. Turn right here onto the PCT and head north.

The trail meanders along at first, near the lake, weaving through a lovely forest of hemlocks with bunchberry, thimbleberry, vanilla

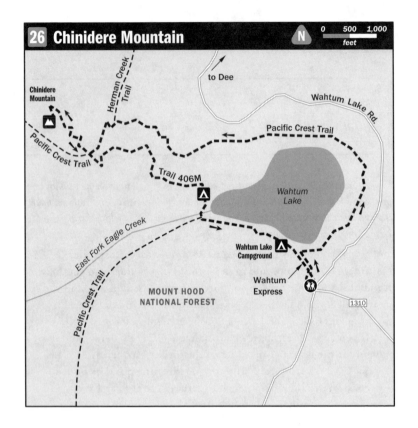

N   0   500   1,000
feet

Chinidere
Mountain

Herman Creek Trail

to Dee

Wahtum Lake Rd.

Pacific Crest Trail

Pacific Crest Trail

Trail 406M

Wahtum
Lake

East Fork Eagle Creek

Wahtum Lake
Campground

Pacific Crest Trail

MOUNT HOOD
NATIONAL FOREST

Wahtum
Express

1310

leaf, columbine, huckleberries, and salmonberry. Look along the near shore for a small island with about four trees on it. Around half a mile up there's also some impressive construction to drain water away from the trail. Tiny springs and mossy, flower-covered babbling brooks entertain and charm in a woodsy manner.

After about 1 flat mile, come into more open forest with bear grass that blooms in July, and begin climbing gradually on some classic Oregon PCT: wide tread, soft ground, pine needles, and thick forest. At 1.75 miles, cross a creek that dries up by midsummer, and at 1.9 miles (now having climbed 400 feet) reach the Herman Creek Trail, which leads all the way down to the outskirts of Cascade Locks.

A tenth of a mile later, look for the Chinidere Cutoff Trail (#406M) plunging down to the left; we'll take that one back. For now, go another 100 feet and leave the PCT on the Chinidere Mountain Trail. Now you'll put in the climbing you've been warming up for, picking up 400 feet in a third of a mile, eventually rounding out onto the rocky summit. You might want to watch for a side trail from one of the first switchbacks, heading out into the open; it leads to a rocky scramble up the west side of the mountain, where you'll find some interesting rock benches made by industrious hikers.

After you've caught your breath, please allow time for a little view tour. Start by looking at Mount Hood, looming to the south. To the right of that is Mount Jefferson, and just to the left of "Jeff" is Olallie Butte. The northbound PCT comes up the right (west) side of Jefferson, around the same side of the butte (where lies Olallie Lake), then past the right side of Hood, mostly in the trees. Just below and to the right of the summit is the Sandy Glacier, source of

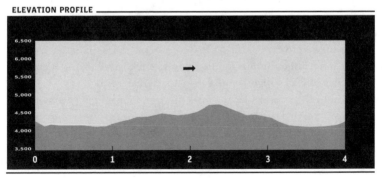

ELEVATION PROFILE

the river that's such an exciting thing for hikers to cross (see the Ramona Falls description) [x-ref].

To the east, beyond Wahtum Lake, look for the upper part of Hood River Valley and to the left of that, Dalles Mountain and the desert of Central Oregon. The big peak with all the radio towers is Mount Defiance, highest spot in the Gorge, and Mount Adams is to its left. The bald ridge directly between you and Adams is Tomlike Mountain (named for Chief Chinidere's son), and left of that is the Herman Creek drainage. Off in the distance are Mounts Rainier and Saint Helens, and right in line with the latter is the broad, flat Benson Plateau. Right below you, to the west, is Eagle Creek Canyon (the East Fork drains Wahtum Lake straight away from your feet) and in the distance beyond that is Tanner Butte. On a really clear day on Chinidere, I was able to see Saddle Mountain, which is about 10 miles this side of the coast!

In its approach to Wahtum Lake, the PCT rounds an open ridge between you and Hood called Indian Mountain, and from Chinidere it heads north across the Benson Plateau and down, heinously, into Cascade Locks. But most thru-hikers take the Eagle Creek Trail—it's well graded and sports about a dozen waterfalls—then walk a few miles along the road into Cascade Locks. (All of this is described in our Eagle Creek–Benson Plateau hike). After crossing the Bridge of the Gods, the trail passes the west side of Table Mountain (which looks like a big gash from Chinidere), then traces around the north side before making a swing east toward Adams, the Goat Rocks, and Rainier. So from Mount Jefferson to Mount Rainier, you're effectively looking at about 280 miles of PCT—slightly more than ten percent of it!

And by the way, the rusty cables on top of Chinidere are from an old Forest Service fire lookout, and the pits are tent sites, not vision-quest sites. Sorry it's nothing more romantic than that.

Now head back down to the PCT, turn left, and take the Chinidere Cutoff Trail, which will seem more like the Chinidere

"Dropoff" Trail as it drops steeply to the lake. You'll cross a creek or two along the way, depending on the season, and you'll even see a pipe along the trail that used to carry water down to some campsites on the north shore of the lake. When you find these campsites, stay on the main trail and follow it to where it crosses the East Fork of Eagle Creek on an impressive (and fun-to-cross) logjam.

Cross the creek, and in 200 yards hit the top of the Eagle Creek National Recreation Trail, which was built before 1920, connecting Wahtum Lake with the Columbia River Highway, 14 miles below. Turn left onto this trail and follow it for about 200 hundred yards back to the PCT, which leads a quarter mile past campsites, swimming holes, and even the occasional beach. Arrive back at the bottom of the Wahtum Express—whose 250 steps will seem much less appealing to you now, no doubt.

DIRECTIONS: From Interstate 84 just west of Hood River, take Exit 62, then take an immediate right onto Country Club Rd., following signs for a bunch of wineries. At the end of Country Club Rd., 3 miles later, turn left at a stop sign onto Barrett Dr. After 1.3 miles, turn right onto Tucker Rd. (the second stop sign you'll come to on Country Club Rd.), which turns into Dee Hwy. Go 8.5 miles to Dee (be sure to make a right that happens 2 miles into this stretch, following signs for Dee and Parkdale) and turn right onto Lost Lake Rd. After 4.8 miles, turn right at a sign for Wahtum Lake onto FS 13. After 4.4 more miles, turn right again, this time onto FS 1310. Stay on the pavement for 6 miles, and look for parking on the right. If you leave the pavement, you've gone too far.

GPS Trailhead Coordinates	26 CHINIDERE MOUNTAIN
UTM zone (WGS84):	10T
Easting:	594165
Northing:	5047815
Latitude:	45°34.650'N
Longitude:	121°47.583'W

27 Eagle Creek *to* Benson Plateau Loop

SCENERY: ☆ ☆ ☆	DISTANCE: *29.2 miles*
TRAIL CONDITION: ☆ ☆ ☆	HIKING TIME: *1 or 2 nights*
CHILDREN: ☆ ☆	OUTSTANDING FEATURES: *An amazing canyon*
DIFFICULTY: ☆ ☆ ☆	*filled with waterfalls, old-growth forest, a high moun-*
SOLITUDE: ☆ ☆	*tain lake, and (later) some solitude.*

When traveling between Wahtum Lake and Cascade Locks, PCT hikers almost always choose the Eagle Creek Trail rather than the PCT—for reasons that will be obvious when you hike it. But why not do both? Make it a long one-nighter or casual two-nighter, and it's a good early- or late-season getaway.

🚶🚶 Let's say you're a long-distance backpacker on the northern-most section of PCT in Oregon. You're either at Wahtum Lake, headed into the town of Cascade Locks to grab a burger, replenish your supplies, and maybe get a ride into Portland, or you're just starting your trip and heading south. Either way, you have two options: the PCT, which is steep and almost viewless, though virtually empty of humanity, and the Eagle Creek Trail, which is a few miles from town and as crowded as anything you'll ever hike, but which includes a dozen or so waterfalls, some spectacular bridges and cliff-side trail sections, and great campsites along a splashing creek.

Which would you take? Well, on this loop you'll do both, so your only choice is which to do first. I prefer going up the more-gradual Eagle Creek Trail and camping one night along it, then spending one night at Wahtum Lake, leaving the dull PCT (about 16 mostly down-hill miles) for the high-speed trek home.

To do this, park at Eagle Creek, but be sure not to leave anything valuable in your car—there have been a lot of break-ins here. I don't even lock my doors at this lot, but I have an old car with a cruddy stereo.

Trail 405E

CASCADE LOCKS
MARINE PARK

Camp Creek

WASHINGTON

Cascade Locks

14

Casey Creek

Wauna
Lake

Cascade
Spring

PCT

30

Herman Creek

84

Benson Plateau

Columbia River

Trail 400

OREGON

Rudolph Creek

Dry Creek

Ruckel Creek

Eagle Creek

Punch Bowl
Falls

MOUNT HOOD
NATIONAL FOREST

Camp Smokey

High
Bridge

Tomike
Mountain

Trail 434

Pacific Crest Trail

4½ Mile
Bridge

Opal Creek

Tunnel
Falls

Wahtum
Lake

Chinidere
Mountain

7½ Mile Camp

Chinidere
Cutoff Trail

Trail 435

Tanner
Butte

Eagle Creek

Indian Springs
Campground

Pacific Crest Trail

Trail 433

DAY
& OVERNIGHT
HIKES

NORTH

part three
MOUNT JEFFERSON TO COLUMBIA RIVER

If you're here in October or November, take a moment to look for Eagle Creek's small run of fall chinook salmon—fish that spend their adult lives in the ocean, come more than 70 miles up the Columbia, swim through the fish ladder at Bonneville Dam, and then come here to spawn. A small dam blocks their further progress up Eagle Creek, but in October and November they spawn in little round pools cleared by volunteers to simulate conditions in a wild mountain stream.

The Eagle Creek Trail is an impressive thing in itself. The work that went into it was a heroic feat: they chipped the trail into cliff faces, built High Bridge over the gorge, and hacked a tunnel behind a falls six miles up.

Just under a mile up, you'll come to the first of several places where you walk a ledge with a cable to hang on to. If it's a summer weekend, things can get interesting here while you're trying to negotiate for cable space with dozens of other hikers. At 1.5 miles, you'll

ELEVATION PROFILE

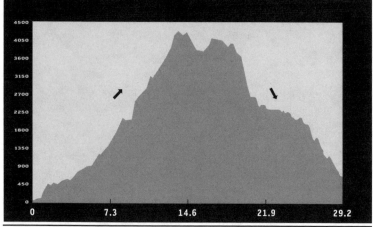

come to a viewpoint of Metlako Falls (named for a native goddess of salmon), the first of many such sights of your day. Just past the viewpoint is a bench for resting. At 1.8 miles and another bench, a side trail leads down to Punchbowl Falls, a must-see trip and the end of the line for a lot of day hikers. Go 0.2 miles down this trail to a large clearing that's often filled with people swimming and sunbathing. At the upstream end of the clearing is a lovely (and often-photographed) view of Punchbowl Falls.

Continuing up, in 0.3 miles you'll get a bird's-eye view of Punchbowl Falls; then the gorge narrows considerably. You'll see Loowit Falls on the right just before High Bridge, and 0.3 miles later come to a great picnic spot and a rare chance for access to the creek itself, in this case at the top of Skooknichuck Falls.

At 4 miles out, you'll cross Four-and-a-Half Mile Bridge. You may wonder, what gives? Well, the fish hatchery back at the trailhead wasn't there when the trail was built (there was no need for it, because Bonneville Dam didn't exist yet), so the trailhead used to be half a mile farther north, at the edge of the Columbia River Highway.

Just past the bridge, look on the right for a double waterfall, and half a mile above that, a sign explains that the area you're now entering was burned in a 1902 fire; there are still some charred stumps around. So all the trees you'll see in this area are less than 100 years old.

After 1.5 more miles, bringing your total to 6, you'll come into a deep gorge where Tunnel Falls plunges 130 feet and the trail goes behind it through a 35-foot tunnel. Tunnel Falls is actually on East Fork Eagle Creek, which drains Wahtum Lake—where you'll be later.

To return to Eagle Creek and see one final, dramatic falls, go about 0.2 miles farther. This falls doesn't have an official name, but it does have an interesting crisscross feature in its upper section, leading many people to call it Crisscross Falls.

The next mile of trail is right along the creek, leading to 7-Mile Camp, which of course is 7 miles from the trailhead. It's a large camping area that would be an excellent place to stop for your first night if you're making the loop over two nights. With a second night at Wahtum Lake or even Benson Plateau, this would leave you plenty of time to kick around Eagle Creek. There are also some campsites between here and Wahtum Lake, which I'll point out as we go.

Beyond the camp, the trail leaves the creek for good and starts two long switchbacks that total 3 miles and gain just 700 feet. At the end of the second switchback, you'll be on the northern end of a spur ridge, with a view back down the canyon. The next 1.6 miles are a bit steeper, but they end at Indian Springs Fork of Eagle Creek, where a nice campsite awaits, a total of 11 miles since the trailhead. Two more miles of gradual climbing past wildflowers, under magnificent trees, and across splashing creeks brings you to the shores of Wahtum Lake, at the head of East Fork Eagle Creek.

Here you have another decision to make. There are campsites right and left, and the PCT is now just 0.1 mile to your right. It's a shorter trip if you go left, and the campsites are less crowded, but it's also steeper going that way. But since going right is basically re-creating the Chinidere Mountain trip described elsewhere in this book, I'll say let's turn left and knock some distance off the hike. (You can still visit Chinidere going this way.)

At the lake's outlet, turn left onto the Chinidere Cutoff Trail and skip across the logjam at the mouth of the creek. Just beyond this is where you'll find several campsites, and then the trail gets steep—some might say darn steep, or even worse. It climbs 600 feet in 0.7 miles, after which you're back on the PCT. Turn left to continue your trip, and in 100 feet you'll see the Chinidere Mountain Trail taking off (and up) to your right. This well-worth-it viewpoint has its own chapter in this book, so I'll refer you to that for the lengthy description.

From here, the PCT takes off north toward the Columbia River. After a mild descent along Chinidere's south side, drop through three saddles, the last of which is called Camp Smokey; as you may guess, there's a campsite here with a spring. You'll also see the top end of the Eagle-Benson Trail, a legendarily steep (and unmaintained) cutoff back to the Eagle Creek Trail. Don't take it, except to reach a better campsite about 200 yards down it, with water 50 yards beyond that.

Leaving the camp, climb for half a mile onto the Benson Plateau, named not for the famous timber man—philanthropist Simon Benson (who gave Portland its famous downtown water fountains) but for a Thomas Benson, an 1864 pioneer from Missouri who lived in Cascade Locks. It is a large, completely forested plateau crisscrossed with trails. The PCT stays on its eastern edge for about 2 miles, passing several variations of Trail 405 along the way. If you want to camp on the plateau, there's a good spot with water about a half mile down Trail 405, which is the second trail you'll reach on the left, halfway along the edge of the plateau.

Leaving the plateau, you'll begin a long, generally viewless descent, losing 2,700 feet over 3.4 miles to a junction with Trail 405E, which cuts 1.8 miles north to the Herman Creek Trailhead. (This is actually a quicker way to the highway than going into Cascade Locks.) After that junction, put in another 2.3 miles to Dry Creek, which isn't, and just past that cross a road you can follow 0.2 miles left to see a 50-foot waterfall.

Truly getting back into civilization now, head 0.7 miles to a power-line road, walk along it for 70 yards, then pick up the PCT for a 1-mile descent to Trail 400, the Gorge Trail. If you're winding up in Cascade Locks, stay on the PCT for a final 0.1 mile, and you'll be in the parking lot for the Bridge of the Gods—which, by the way, is how PCT through-hikers get over the Columbia, believe it or not.

If you're coming out at Eagle Creek, turn left on Trail 400, and it will more or less parallel Interstate 84 for 2.5 miles back to the Eagle Creek Trailhead.

DIRECTIONS: From Portland on I-84, drive 34 miles east of I-205 and take Exit 41/Eagle Creek. Go 0.2 miles and turn right, then 0.6 miles to the end of the road. If it's crowded, you might have to park closer to the highway and hike that much farther.

GPS Trailhead Coordinates	27 EAGLE CREEK TO BENSON PLATEAU LOOP
UTM Zone (WGS84):	10T
Easting:	583862
Northing:	5054601
Latitude:	45°38.393'N
Longitude:	121°55.435'W

Appendix A: Hikes by Category

DAY OUT-AND-BACKS (*some may also be overnights*)
   1   California Border to Observation Peak
   2   Grouse Gap to Siskiyou Peak
   3   OR 99 to Pilot Rock
   5   OR 62 to Pumice Flats
   6   OR 62 to Crater Lake Rim
   7   Crater Lake Rim
   10 Rosary Lakes to Maiden Peak Shelter
   13 Lava Camp Lake to Collier Glacier View
   14 Little Belknap Crater
   17 Jefferson Park
   18 Breitenbush Lake to Park Butte
   19 Olallie Lake to Upper Lake
   20 Little Crater Lake to Timothy Lake
   22 Barlow Pass to Timberline Lodge
   25 Lost Lake to Buck Peak

DAY LOOPS (*some may also be overnights*)
   4   Sky Lakes Wilderness
   15 Three-Fingered Jack
   21 Twin Lakes Loop
   23 Timberline Lodge to Paradise Park
   24 Ramona Falls to Sandy River Loop
   26 Chinidere Mountain

OVERNIGHT HIKES (*some may also be done as day hikes*)
   4   Sky Lakes Wilderness
   6   OR 62 to Crater Lake Rim
   8   Mount Thielsen Loop

Appendix B: First-aid Kit

A typical first-aid kit may contain more items than you might think necessary. These are just the basics. Prepackaged kits in waterproof bags (Atwater Carey and Adventure Medical make a variety of kits) are available. Even though there are quite a few items listed here, they pack down into a small space:

Ace bandages or Spence joint wraps

Antibiotic ointment (Neosporin or the generic equivalent)

Aspirin or acetaminophen

Band-Aids

Benadryl or the generic equivalent diphenhydramine (in case of allergic reactions)

Butterfly-closure bandages

Epinephrine in a prefilled syringe (for people known to have severe allergic reactions to such things as bee stings)

Gauze (one roll)

Gauze compress pads (a half dozen 4- x 4-inch pads)

Hydrogen peroxide or iodine

Insect repellent

Matches or pocket lighter

Moleskin/Spenco "Second Skin"

Sunscreen

Whistle (it's more effective in signaling rescuers than your voice)

Appendix C: Contacts

USDA FOREST SERVICE—PACIFIC NORTHWEST REGION
333 SW First Avenue
Portland, OR 97208-3623
(503) 808-2468
www.fs.fed.us/r6

PACIFIC CREST TRAIL ASSOCIATION
www.pcta.org
5325 Elkhorn Boulevard, PMB# 256
Sacramento, CA 95842-2526
(916) 349-2109
Toll-free trail conditions: (888) 728-7245

BUREAU OF LAND MANAGEMENT
www.blm.gov/or/districts/medford/index.htm

Medford District
3040 Biddle Road
Medford, OR 97504
(541) 618-2200

Rogue-Siskiyou National Forest
www.fs.fed.us/r6/rogue-siskiyou
Supervisor's Office
333 West Eighth Street
Medford, OR 97501-0209
(541) 858-2200

Applegate Ranger District
6941 Upper Applegate Road
Jacksonville, OR 97530-9314
(541) 899-3800

Butte Falls Ranger District
47201 OR 62
Prospect, OR 97536-9724
(541) 865-2700

Ashland Ranger District
645 Washington Street
Ashland, OR 97520-1402
(541) 552-2900

UMPQUA NATIONAL FOREST
www.fs.fed.us/r6/umpqua

Supervisor's Office
2900 NW Stewart Parkway
Roseburg, OR 97470
(541) 672-6601

Diamond Lake Ranger District
2020 Toketee RS Road
Idleyld Park, OR 97447
(541) 498-2531

CRATER LAKE NATIONAL PARK
www.nps.gov/crla
Supervisor's Office
P.O. Box 7
Crater Lake, OR 97604
(541) 594-3000

Deschutes National Forest
www.fs.fed.us/r6/centraloregon

Supervisor's Office
1001 SW Emkay Drive
Bend, OR 97702
(541) 383-5300

Bend–Fort Rock Ranger District
1230 NE Third Street, Suite A-262
Bend, OR 97701
(541) 383-4000

Crescent Ranger District
136471 Highway 97 N
Crescent, OR 97733
(541) 433-3200

Sisters Ranger District
Pine Street and Highway 20
Sisters, OR 97759
(541) 549-7700

Willamette National Forest
www.fs.fed.us/r6/willamette

Supervisor's Office
211 East Seventh Avenue
Eugene, OR 97401
(541) 225-6300

Detroit Ranger District
P.O. Box 320
Mill City, OR 97360
(503) 854-3366

McKenzie River Ranger District
57600 McKenzie Highway
McKenzie Bridge, OR 97413
(541) 822-3381

Mount Hood National Forest
www.fs.fed.us/r6/mthood
Supervisor's Office
16400 Champion Way
Sandy, OR 97055
(503) 668-1700

Hood River Ranger District
6780 Highway 35
Parkdale, OR 97041
(541) 352-6002

Zigzag Ranger District
70220 East Highway 26
Zigzag, OR 97049
(503) 622-3191

Clackamas River Ranger District
595 NW Industrial Way
Estacada, OR 97023
(503) 630-6861

Columbia River Gorge NSA
902 Wasco Street, Suite 200
Hood River, OR 97031
(541) 308-1700
www.fs.fed.us/r6/columbia

Contact Info for Hikes

Index

About the Author

One day, Paul Gerald was sitting in his cubicle at a highly respected insurance company when the phone rang. It was a good friend inviting him on a walk across Oregon on the Pacific Crest Trail. A few months later, Paul was unemployed and sleeping in the woods—just the way he likes it.

It's not like he was a "career guy" when that phone rang. He grew up in Memphis and developed early addictions to both hiking and traveling. He got the journalism bug while at Southern Methodist University in the 1980s and went on to work in the sports departments of the *Dallas Times-Herald* and the *Memphis Commercial Appeal*. He was also a staff writer for the *Memphis Flyer*, and to this day, some ten years and three hundred columns later, he remains their travel writer. He moved to Portland in 1996 because it's a whole lot closer to mountains, old forests, clear rivers, and lonesome ocean beaches. Along the way, he has also written for Portland's *Willamette Week*, the *Oregonian*, and all sorts of newspapers, magazines, and Web sites around the country. And to avoid doing any settled kind of work, he has also dabbled in commercial fishing, landscaping, social work, the YMCA, and an amusement park.

Today, he is still a freelance writer specializing in his three passions—food, the outdoors, and travel. He is also the author of Menasha Ridge Press's *60 Hikes within 60 Miles: Portland*, the third edition of which came out in spring 2007.

To keep up with Paul and contact him, visit him online at **www.paulgerald.com**.

DEAR CUSTOMERS AND FRIENDS,

SUPPORTING YOUR INTEREST IN OUTDOOR ADVENTURE, travel, and an active lifestyle is central to our operations, from the authors we choose to the locations we detail to the way we design our books. Menasha Ridge Press was incorporated in 1982 by a group of veteran outdoorsmen and professional outfitters. For 25 years now, we've specialized in creating books that benefit the outdoors enthusiast.

Almost immediately, Menasha Ridge Press earned a reputation for revolutionizing outdoors- and travel-guidebook publishing. For such activities as canoeing, kayaking, hiking, backpacking, and mountain biking, we established new standards of quality that transformed the whole genre, resulting in outdoor-recreation guides of great sophistication and solid content. Menasha Ridge continues to be outdoor publishing's greatest innovator.

The folks at Menasha Ridge Press are as at home on a white-water river or mountain trail as they are editing a manuscript. The books we build for you are the best they can be, because we're responding to your needs. Plus, we use and depend on them ourselves.

We look forward to seeing you on the river or the trail. If you'd like to contact us directly, join in at www.trekalong.com or visit us at www.menasharidge.com. We thank you for your interest in our books and the natural world around us all.

SAFE TRAVELS,

Bob Sehlinger

BOB SEHLINGER
PUBLISHER